DOORWAY TO A NEW AGE

DOORWAY TO A NEW AGE

A Study
of Paul's Letter
to the Romans

JAMES D. SMART

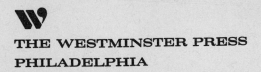

THE WESTMINSTER PRESS
PHILADELPHIA

Scripture quotations from the Revised Standard
Version of the Bible are copyright, 1946 and
1952, by the Division of Christian Education
of the National Council of Churches,
and are used by permission.

PUBLISHED BY THE WESTMINSTER PRESS®
PHILADELPHIA, PENNSYLVANIA

PRINTED IN THE UNITED STATES OF AMERICA

Library of Congress Cataloging in Publication Data

Smart, James D.
  Doorway to a new age.

  Bibliography: p.
  1. Bible. N. T. Romans—Criticism, interpretation,
etc. I. Title.
BS2665.2.S6   1975   227'.1'066   74–8559
ISBN 0–664–24997–3

To my colleagues
on the faculty of
Union Theological Seminary,
New York, 1957-71.

CONTENTS

PREFACE

Much of the language of the letter to the Romans weighs heavily on the mind at a first reading but, as we read and reread it, gradually working our way into the mind of the apostle, the words begin to come alive and the text which at first weighed us down begins to lift us up and carry us into new regions of thought and life.

The study of Romans is like a walking tour in a mountainous country where one first toils laboriously upward with little compensation but after a time is rewarded with vistas that would otherwise have been impossible to gain. But let the reader take warning: it is Paul's letter that takes us up the mountainside and into these new regions. The commentary alone will not do it. The commentary is no more than a staff to lean on or a guide-book to point out things that might otherwise be missed. It is from the Letter alone that the vistas open out to be seen and experienced. Paul's letter to the Romans must be read, reread, and pondered until it ceases to be a letter to some Roman Christians of long ago and becomes a personal letter from Paul to you.

More than once in the past this letter to the Romans has led Christians to rediscover the power of the New Testament faith to shake their world and to transform it. For Luther, for John Wesley, for Karl Barth, and many others, it has been the point at which the whole Bible began to come open to them in a new way and what they heard from it has changed the course of Christian and social history. The hope with which this guide-book goes forth is that it may provide the necessary help for Christians today to make the same kind of discovery and experience for themselves the same humbling and life-transforming power of the Gospel.

Without this fresh and continuous discovery the church will be helpless when confronted with the varied and exacting challenges of the contemporary world.

James D. Smart

"Faith is a divine work in us, which changes us and makes us newly born of God, and kills the old Adam, makes us completely different men in heart, disposition, mind and every power, and brings the Holy Spirit with it. O, faith is a lively, creative, active, powerful thing, so that it is impossible that it should not continually do good works. It does not even ask if good works are to be done, but before anyone asks it has done them, and is always acting."

MARTIN LUTHER'S PREFACE TO HIS
COMMENTARY ON THE EPISTLE TO THE ROMANS

"By a Christian I mean one who so believes (has faith) in Christ that sin has no more dominion over him; and in this sense of the word I was not a Christian until May 24 past [1738]. While attending a prayer group in Aldersgate Street, an assurance was given me that He had taken away my sins, even mine, and saved me from the law of sin and death. . . . I felt myself gripped with a new power, my heart was strangely warmed. I felt that now I really believed and trusted in Christ and Christ alone for my salvation. . . . I now had faith and courage and a heightened sense of responsibility for my fellow men which has never ceased to develop."

JOHN WESLEY'S JOURNAL,
AFTER HEARING THE PREFACE OF
LUTHER'S COMMENTARY ON ROMANS

"He who accepts Romans: 1:18—3:20, saying, 'Yes, I am that man!' shall hear this: 'You are the man whom God has justified!' And again he shall answer: 'Yes, I am this man! this man I am allowed to be and I desire to be.' " *

KARL BARTH'S
A SHORTER COMMENTARY ON ROMANS

---

* Used by permission of John Knox Press.

MORE THAN ONCE IN THE PAST THIS LETTER TO THE ROMANS HAS LED CHRISTIANS TO REDISCOVER THE POWER OF THE NEW TESTAMENT FAITH TO SHAKE THEIR WORLD AND TO TRANSFORM IT. [x]

PAUL'S LETTER TO THE ROMANS MUST BE READ, REREAD, AND PONDERED UNTIL IT CEASES TO BE A LETTER TO SOME ROMAN CHRISTIANS OF LONG AGO AND BECOMES A PERSONAL LETTER FROM PAUL TO YOU! [x]

PAUL NOT ONLY WAS A MISSIONARY TO THE GENTILES, BUT IN ORDER TO CARRY OUT HIS MISSION HE RE-EXPRESSED THE GOSPEL IN A LANGUAGE AND IN TERMS WHICH THEY COULD FIND MEANINGFUL. [5]

A SAINT IS ANYONE WHOSE LIFE (ALTHOUGH STILL IMPERFECT) IS MADE HOLY BY THE INDWELLING PRESENCE OF GOD'S HOLY SPIRIT. [6]

ALL EVENTS TAKE ON NEW SIGNIFICANCE WHEN MEN AND WOMEN ARE AT PEACE WITH GOD. [27]

WHAT GOD'S PROMISE FORESHADOWED IN ABRAHAM IS FULFILLED ON BEHALF OF ALL PEOPLE IN THE DEATH AND RESURRECTION OF JESUS (ROM. 4). [26]

chapter I
WHY PAUL?

Many people today are discouraged when they first try to read Paul's letters. They ask, "Why read Paul when we can go to the very heart of the Christian faith, to Jesus himself, in the Gospels? And, does not Paul use difficult, complicated words and abstract theological phrases in strong contrast to the simple, vivid language and truth-revealing stories of Jesus?"

Some even express the suspicion that Paul took a simple gospel of Jesus and, in interpreting it for the Gentile world, encumbered it with a host of ideas and doctrinal developments which have been a burden to the Christian faith ever since. One scholar[1] has even called Paul a "second founder of Christianity" who ignored the teachings of Jesus and developed a religion around the figure of Jesus as a heavenly Lord.

The belief that the four Gospels take us closer in time to the Event in which Christianity had its birth than do the letters of Paul, is really an illusion. The Event includes more than the mission of Jesus, his preaching, teaching, healing, and exorcising (driving out) demons. It also includes his death and resurrection and his continuing presence with his disciples through their remembrance of him and their receiving of his Spirit. No one, it seems, made an immediate record of what happened. Jesus wrote nothing, nor is there convincing evidence that any of the disciples with him in his lifetime wrote down an account of what they saw and heard. The sayings of Jesus and brief stories of his actions, however, were used in Christian worship and in the instruction of converts, and began very early to develop into Christian traditions, the earliest and most vivid tradition being the account of Jesus' death and resurrection. It is very difficult to determine when these oral traditions became written documents. Eventually, in different sections of the church, they were shaped into Gospels—the Gospel of Mark in the late sixties, the others nearer to the end of the century. While all the Gospels contain sayings that are the very words of Jesus, each of them as a whole is an interpretation of Jesus and his gospel, made by an author who was farther from Jesus in time and in other ways than Paul. No less than Paul, each Gospel author also had his own theological perspective, or point of view.[2] This is most recognizable in the Gospel of John, but is equally true of others. In short, our access to Jesus is through the recorded witness of a number of interpreters whose writings form the New Testament. Paul, however, seems to be the first of them to have put his witness into writing.

Paul began his witness early. His first letter to the Thessalonians was written in A.D. 53, some fifteen years before the Gospel of Mark. He is also the only New Testament author who can claim to have received his gospel in direct personal confrontation with Jesus Christ himself according to his account of the experience on the road to Damascus, (Gal. 1:12, compare Acts 9). All others are dependent on traditions. The author of Luke-Acts makes his distance from the original events very clear in Luke 1:1-4. He has before him a number of accounts of Jesus' ministry which he describes as having been handed down from "eye-witnesses and ministers of the word." One such account that he used was the Gospel of Mark, which was itself a composite made up of earlier traditions. In contrast to this, Paul stands *within* the original Event itself.

There is no evidence that he ever saw or heard Jesus before his crucifixion, but soon afterward he knew enough about him to become a persecutor of his followers and thereby, in a real sense, a participant in his continuing crucifixion. He knew even more profoundly than Peter or John the darkness of the Cross and then the blinding yet transforming light of the Resurrection. What would we not give to have in our hands a letter from Peter or John about what the cross and resurrection of Jesus meant to them? *But we have such a letter from Paul!* Across the centuries Paul speaks to us and shares with us in the profoundest way his understanding and experience of the impact of Jesus Christ upon his life and that of the world.

But Paul's language (Greek) was neither the Aramaic language of Jesus nor our most familiar language, English. Coming to us through various translations, it inevitably creates obstacles to our understanding and fails to communicate easily its original meaning directly to us. Jesus never moved out of the tiny, Aramaic-speaking Palestinian Jewish world. He confined his mission largely to the "lost sheep of the house of Israel," to Jews who, for one reason or another, no longer regarded themselves as participants in the faith of Israel. Although he grew up in the strictest sect of the Jewish religion, Paul was a citizen of the Roman empire and spoke Greek fluently. He was convinced that his assignment and commission from the risen Lord was to be an apostle to carry the gospel to the Gentile world. Paul spoke to a completely different cultural and religious situation than did Jesus.

Jesus, a man of the common people, spoke their language and used the familiar scenes of everyday life in his teaching and preaching: sowing seed, patching garments, fishing, building houses, the traveller robbed on his journey, the wayward son returning home, persons hopelessly in debt, a widow nagging a judge to right a wrong, mustard seeds and wildflowers. But Paul, a man of the schools, a trained rabbi, used a more scholarly language which had its own virtues but none of the homeliness and familiarity of Jesus' speech. The monumental significance of Paul's achievement, however, lies in the fact that he translated a gospel which was born and first came to expression in a purely Jewish setting (and in the next generation was, therefore, in danger of being misunderstood), into language and thought forms that would be more universally comprehensible and understandable in the larger, wider, more sophisticated Hellenistic world of Greeks and Romans. Paul not only was a missionary to the Gentiles, but in order to carry out his mission he re-expressed the gospel in a language and in terms which they could find meaningful.

Just as the language of Jesus was unfamiliar to Greeks and Romans, much of the language of Paul is unfamiliar to us. For many people reading a book such as Romans today is like reading a book sprinkled with phrases in Latin, French, or some even less familiar language. Not only are such terms as 'justification,' 'righteousness of God,' 'expiation,' unfamiliar to us, but even familiar words such as 'servant' and 'saint' had quite different meanings for Paul than they have for us. We often think of someone employed at household tasks as a servant, or—in a political sense—we speak of a servant of the people; but never do we consider that the term translated 'servant' denotes a binding relationship. But the word used by Paul also means 'slave' and denotes one completely, permanently, bound to a master.

'Saint' suggests to us someone who has reached perfection in character and is free of all sin, but when Paul addresses the members of his churches as 'saints,' he is not attributing to them any such perfection. For Paul, a saint is anyone whose life (although still imperfect) is made holy by the indwelling presence of God's Holy Spirit. In chapters 2 and 3 of Romans he makes us emphatically aware that all the saints are sinners!

Paul's term 'righteousness of God' has a highly complex meaning, yet an understanding of that meaning is essential for an understanding of Paul's thought in Romans. This and other terms such as 'justification by faith' simply cannot be understood with a quick superficial reading of the text. Such terms must be studied, thought about, pondered.

In the early stages of Martin Luther's life as a monk these terms conjured up in his imagination a righteous God before whom he was terrified, a God whose righteousness he could never satisfy by even the most severe of his penances. But after much agonizing questioning and thought he came to understand from this letter to the Romans that these words signify a righteousness which God in his love imparts, bestows as a gift, through Jesus Christ, to the sinful man in order to purge away his sins. These became Luther's best-loved words, bringing him infinite comfort and assurance. We could have no better warning than this to show us how extremely important it is for us to go behind Paul's words and into the depth of their meaning, which often does not quickly show itself on the surface. Paul's words are to be read slowly, thoughtfully, with the help of the church's scholarship and with the prayer that God reveal their real and deepest meanings to us. Then we, in turn, may help others find their transforming power, as did Martin Luther and John Wesley.

PAUL IN ACTS AND IN THE LETTERS

To truly understand Paul, we must draw our primary picture from his letters rather than from the narrative of Acts. Acts enlarges the picture and is a history written a full generation after Paul's death. It uses traditional material about him that was preserved by several early churches and perhaps in notes in the travel diary of a companion on some of his journeys. But the letters are from Paul himself. (Most scholars are agreed that Romans, I and II Corinthians, Galatians, Philippians, and I Thessalonians, were written by Paul and that the other letters were composed by persons who were close to him.) The letters then, are the primary source for a knowledge of Paul and material in Acts is secondary. If the letters and Acts disagree at any point, we shall therefore give the greater weight to Paul's own statements in his letters.[3]

Too often this is directly opposite to the way most Bible readers approach Paul. First, they become familiar with the story of Paul in Acts.

(Many never get beyond the Acts to the letters.) If we were to question the graduates of our church schools, we would probably find that they know something of Paul's conversion and missionary journeys but very little about his doctrine of *justification by faith*. Many of them are far more familiar with Paul the missionary traveler and the founder of churches than with Paul the preacher, teacher, critical theologian, and strong champion of Christian freedom.

If we had only the Book of Acts and none of Paul's letters, we would have no knowledge of the battle he waged for the freedom of the gospel. The author of Acts looks back at the beginnings of the church from near the end of the first century; for him all the separate strands which made up the life of that church are blended closely together. He sees the Jerusalem church as all of one piece, with Stephen and his fellow Hellenists (Greek-speaking Jewish Christians) merely deacons in the church of the Twelve. Peter and Paul, the outstanding leaders, are pictured as very much alike in their preaching and actions. Peter in Acts even precedes Paul as a missionary to the Gentiles. Differences which existed between Paul and the Jerusalem church seem to be very easily settled. But when one begins with Paul's letters, then digs beneath the surface in

Acts, the story of the early church takes on a somewhat different character.[4]

A more careful eye observes that the original disciples were not at all ready for a mission to the Gentile world. When Peter baptized Cornelius and his household (he was persuaded to do so only by a special vision) his action was severely criticized by a section of the Jerusalem church.[5] For that group the church was a Jewish church, and membership in it required that a Gentile become a Jew and conform to basic Jewish practices. Had not Jesus earlier told his disciples to go only to "the lost sheep of the house of Israel"?

Then when we turn to Paul's Letter to the Galatians, we find how large a problem this question had become in Paul's new churches and how Paul insisted that the gospel must break out of its Jewish setting and be offered freely to all men. Jewish Christians might still be circumcised and observe the kosher food laws, but these observances must not be required of Gentiles, nor should Jewish Christians let their absence become a barrier to fellowship and sitting at table with Gentile Christians. In Antioch, where the church was composed of both Jews and Gentiles, Paul's viewpoint prevailed at first and Peter, who was present, shared in this pioneering venture in Christian unity. But the more conservative church in Jerusalem, under the leadership of James, the brother of Jesus, was so disturbed by reports of this development in the Antioch church that it sent messengers to demand that Jewish Christians must observe the strict Jewish food laws and must not eat with Gentiles. To Paul's dismay even Peter obeyed the order, and the community was split in two." James and Peter were agreed that Gentiles should be free of such Jewish regulations, but there were others in Jerusalem and elsewhere who tried to force the Jewish practices on all Gentile converts. Paul fought this battle on behalf of the Gentiles in order that they, and we today, might have free access to the faith and the life which are the gift of God in Jesus Christ. Had he not fought and won, Christianity could have remained only a special sect in Judaism. This crucial issue in the life of the early church is an important element in the background of the Letter to the Romans since the traditions of the Jerusalem church seem to have exerted a strong influence very early on the Roman church. Today we face the same choice between loyalty to old customs and freedom for new developments as we meet new groups and new problems.

The Book of Acts makes Paul subordinate to

the Jerusalem apostles. It indicates that only the apostles who were disciples in Jesus' lifetime were in the first rank.[7] Paul, as an apostle of the Antioch church, was thus excluded from the first rank. But Paul insists in Galatians ch. 1 (and elsewhere) that he is in no way inferior to the Twelve. He declares that he, too, is a witness to the risen Lord, having received both the gospel and the commission as apostle to the Gentiles directly from Jesus.[8] Although Acts represents Paul as having gone to Jerusalem shortly after his conversion to consult with the Twelve and to be accepted by them.[9] Paul writes that he did not go up to Jerusalem immediately after his conversion; that he was three years an apostle before he visited Jerusalem, and on that occasion he saw only Peter and James. His next visit was fourteen years later when controversy concerning his gospel made him decide to consult again with Peter and James to see whether his preaching of Christ crucified and risen differed in any serious way from theirs. Not only was he reassured that he, Peter, and James, preached essentially the same gospel, but it was then agreed between them that he should have the primary responsibility for the Gentile missions while Peter would be primarily missionary to the Jewish diaspora (the Jews outside of Palestine).[10] In the light of this agreement

Paul was doubly distressed and angry when Peter drew back and refused to let Jewish Christians sit at the table in fellowship with Gentiles at Antioch. Paul and Peter were close enough to each other in their understanding of the gospel to share freely for a time in the work of the Antioch mission, but at this one point Peter was not as ready as was Paul for the gospel to break out of its Jewish cocoon and spread its wings in the wider context of all humanity.

There are other points of difference between the Acts and the letters in reference to Paul. Of major concern is the description of his preaching to the Gentiles.[11] Only two examples of it are given, neither of them more than a fragment (Acts. 14:15-17 and 17:22-31). What strikes us most forcibly in these two passages is the absence of any mention of Christ crucified. Typical of the doctrine in the letters is Paul's assertion (I Cor. 2:2) that when he arrived among the Corinthian Gentiles, he determined to know nothing and to preach nothing "except Jesus Christ and him crucified." The good news of the gospel was that in the death and resurrection of Jesus the power of God had broken in upon mankind to put an end to an old death-bound world and to create not merely new men but a new world. In Acts 14:15-17, however, the good news is that the time has come for all men to put aside their idols and turn to the living God who made heaven and earth. In Acts 17:22-31 almost the whole sermon at Athens is an appeal to turn from the worship of idols or "an unknown God" to worship God the creator, by whose bounty all men have life. The appeal was sharpened by the warning that the day of judgment was approaching. Jesus appears in the sermon only as "a man whom he [God] has appointed" to execute his judgment upon the world, and the reference to the Resurrection of Jesus in the closing sentence interprets that event only as God's assurance to man that Jesus is to be his judge in the last day.

It can scarcely be argued that this was Paul's customary way of preaching to Gentiles. Some scholars maintain that it represents one approach Paul may have sometimes made; others feel that the author of Acts, never having heard Paul preach, attributed to him an approach familiar in the church of his own post-apostolic time. Certainly if we want to know how Paul preached we should let him tell us himself. We should not let the representation of Paul's preaching in Acts stand as a shield between us and the more incisive confrontation with Christ crucified and risen that Paul himself provides for us in his letters.

Having questioned the presentation of Paul in Acts, we must emphasize all the more the enormous, inestimable value of the Book of Acts to the church. It may be fragmentary and overly conciliatory in some respects, concealing the sharp divisions in the early church, but it alone pictures for us the life of that church. It binds the two halves of the New Testament into one. Without it the New Testament falls into two parts—the four Gospels, on the one hand, and a bundle of letters plus Revelations, on the other. The Book of Acts provides a rich background for understanding both the Gospels and the letters. If it is read superficially, Acts can leave us with an overly simplified view of the early church, but read attentively with thought and care, it becomes a rich mine of information. Its author was himself an able theologian who laid the foundation for the ongoing missionary enterprise of the church. He unfolded the story of the Christian faith from its beginnings, from the births of John the Baptist and Jesus, to its arrival with Paul at the capital city of the Roman empire. The author of Acts is criticized at some points because his account of Paul was dependent upon inadequate traditions, or incomplete reports. We should fully recognize, however, that Paul was his missionary-hero, much more so even than Peter.

We are indebted to him for the valuable biographical information and the universal missionary perspective which he alone provides.

There are other reasons why Paul's letter to the Romans has played a very important part throughout the history of the church. If we will let it, it can again. That it stands first in the collection of Paul's letters is due not just to its length, but to the fact that it is the most ordered, complete, and comprehensive statement of the gospel as Paul understood it. As such it stands alone in the New Testament. It must have been largely responsible for the influence which Paul continued to exercise in the church of the early centuries.

A most dramatic instance of the remarkable power of Paul's letter to the Romans to cut through the confusion of men's minds, to restore an understanding of what God did and continues to do for mankind in Jesus Christ, is found in the sixteenth century Reformation. That great Renewal of the church began when Martin Luther, then a professor of Bible in an Augustinian seminary at Wittenberg, Germany, read the letter to the Romans with his students and began to clear away the mass of misinterpretations that had been heaped upon it. As they read together their minds began to grasp the original meaning. Only gradually did Luther himself recognize the revolutionary significance of what he was reading. First there came a marvelous liberation of his own soul from its agonies of doubt and confusion and his Christian life was established upon a solid and enduring ground. Soon, however, he became aware of point after point at which the contemporary establishment, teaching, and practices of the church, were in glaring contradiction to the gospel which he rediscovered first in Romans and then in the whole of the Scriptures.

Two centuries later a group of earnest people in London, England, troubled by the low condition into which the church had fallen and the resulting weakness in its spiritual life, were gathered in a house on Aldersgate Street to listen to a reading of Luther's commentary on Paul's letter to the Romans. John Wesley was present that evening and, as he listened, his heart was "strangely warmed." Paul's words, interpreted by Luther, brought alive for him the transforming power of the gospel and gave him confidence that the new age which Paul had seen dawning for all mankind in Jesus Christ could certainly be a new age for England.

Again, in our own century the letter to the

Romans has provoked revolutionary changes in Christian theology and in significant areas of the church's life. During World War I a young Swiss pastor and theologian, Karl Barth, found the whole understanding of the gospel in which he had been trained disastrously weak and confused in the face of the urgent problems confronting humanity. What distressed him most was how the Christian faith was subtly, and usually unconsciously, blended with the national culture, so that the virtues of the culture and the virtues of the Christian faith were seen as one. This tended to reinforce the self-confidence of modern man rather than to bring him and his whole way of life under judgment and to repentance. In this union of faith and national culture, faith lost its cutting edge. It was being used as a spiritual enhancement of Western civilization, instead of being the redemptive salt that could save the West from self-destruction. Barth, like Luther, first had to find his own way to a rediscovery of the gospel. During the years 1914-18, while Europe was engulfed in war, he worked his way—in private study and public preaching and teaching—through most of Paul's letters. In his struggle to understand Paul, Barth hammered out a commentary on Romans which he published in 1918,[12] but, dissatisfied with what he had written, again went to work on what became an almost totally new book published in 1922.[13] This second commentary on Romans set men to rethinking their approach to the Scriptures and their understanding of the Christian faith. The existence of a confessional church in Germany which gave some degree of resistance to the Nazi Germanization of the church in the thirties was in no small degree a consequence of Barth's commentary on Romans! The effects were felt far beyond Germany.

The eminent English Methodist scholar, C. K. Barrett, in the preface to his own commentary on Romans, says of Barth's commentary, "If in those days [of World War II], and since, I remained and have continued to be a Christian, I owe the fact in large measure to that book, and to those in Cambridge who introduced it to me."[14] Many others could pay the same tribute. Its influence and impact upon biblical scholars and theologians of the most divergent viewpoints, both Protestant and Catholic, has been immense. It is not that they were made "Barthians," but that they were provoked to listen in a new, fresh, and direct way to Paul. And that they found through Paul a clearer, more vital, comprehension of the deepest meaning, not only of the whole of the New Testament but also of the Old Testament.

We ask why Paul, particularly in his letter to the Romans, has more than once provided this re-entry into the meaning and message of the Scriptures. As has been said earlier in this chapter, where other writers preserved for us the church's traditions concerning the Christ Event, *Paul speaks to us from within the Event itself.* Where the Gospels in their transmission and re-telling may have gathered a certain amount of additional or legendary material which tends to obscure their original intent and meaning, Paul's writing is free from such elements. In spite of the nineteen centuries which lie between his lifetime and ours, he still speaks directly to us as person to person. An Old Testament parallel is seen in Elijah and Amos. Elijah comes to us in a series of popular traditions in which the legendary elements are visible, though they do not hide his stature as a prophet. But Amos' words, preserved almost intact by his disciples, are totally free from such added elements. Once we understand his historical situation, Amos speaks for us as a man of only yesterday. Paul for the same reason steps more easily than any other New Testament author into our modern world to be our guide into the meaning of the Christ Event.

In reading a letter, we like to know as much as possible about both the sender and the receiver and also about what occasioned the letter. Paul was born in Tarsus in Asia Minor but he seems to have moved to Jerusalem at an early age and to have grown up there, eventually being trained as a rabbi in the school of Gamaliel.[15] He excelled most of his contemporaries in religious devotion and zeal for the faith of his fathers. There is no evidence that he was ever in contact with Jesus before the crucifixion. However, Paul quickly recognized the new Christian movement to be a serious threat to the future of Judaism. He therefore became a vehement persecutor of the Christians. This role ended, and, his life as a Christian apostle began, when, near Damascus, he had a vision of the risen Christ and, receiving new life from God through Him, became a missionary of the faith whose adherents he had been persecuting!

After passing some time in a region of Arabia East of Damascus (perhaps to think through the meaning of what had happened to him), Paul spent three years in Damascus. Following a brief visit to Jerusalem to talk with Peter and James, and to escape the dangers which threatened his life in Palestine and Syria, he returned to Tarsus where he spent some years of which we have no record.

He comes more clearly into the light in Antioch where refugees from Jerusalem had established a church with both Jews and Gentiles in it. This pioneering venture needed leadership and it was natural that Paul with his commitment to carry the gospel to the Gentile world should be drawn from Tarsus to Antioch. But Antioch was to be only the first stage of a world mission. Sharing Paul's vision, the church before long sent him westward on the first of his missionary journeys with Barnabas and Mark as his companions, though the freedom of his approach to Gentiles was soon to separate them from him.

Paul's travels eventually took him to the western limits of Asia Minor and then across the Hellespont into Europe. Wherever he went he planted churches. He met resistance both from his fellow Jews and from the adherents of native religions, and in some places he was severely beaten. Most painful of all, he had to endure attacks on his churches and on himself by fellow Christians who identified a genuine Christianity with its earliest Jewish form and regarded him as a falsifier of the gospel. Paul, therefore, not only had to establish his churches but as he moved on he had to send messengers and letters back to them to protect them from being misled. Some of his strongest churches were established in Greece at Philippi, Thessalonica, and Corinth. At Corinth he spent some years and his letters to the Corinthians bring their church vividly before us. It is most likely while he was at Corinth that he wrote his letter to the church at Rome.

Troubled by the division between Jewish and Gentile Christians, Paul must often have pondered what could be done to heal the rift. For him there could be only one Church, one body of Christ. When a famine in Palestine reduced many of the Christians there to abject poverty he determined to collect a fund from his Gentile churches for their relief as a sign of the unity of the Christian fellowship. He saw this also as the climax of his work in Asia Minor and Greece. He was able to say, ". . . from Jerusalem and as far round as Illyricum I have fully preached the gospel of Christ . . ." (Rom. 15:19).

Now Paul's mind was reaching out to the other half of the Roman world—to Italy and the western region as far as Spain (Rom. 15:24). First he had to deliver his famine fund to Jerusalem. Then he would be free to begin his mission in the West—not in Rome, but in the farthest limits of the West, in Spain where as yet there were no Christians. Just as Antioch had been the home base for the first stage of the Gentile mission, it was now natural that Rome should be the home base for the second stage. The letter to Rome was, therefore, a strategic step in preparing the way for this new venture.

It is clear from the letter that the church was already securely established in Rome. Who its founders were is wholly unknown. There was a constant movement of people between the East and Rome for various reasons—business, administrative, religious. Jewish pilgrims from Jerusalem to Rome may have been the carriers of the new faith. Converts from Greece or Asia Minor may have moved to Rome. The church was primarily Gentile in character, but chapters 2-3 and 9-11 of Romans suggest the presence of a strong Jewish influence and a considerable body of Jews among its members. Paul tries hard to make it very plain that to be a Christian is to be most truly a Jew—but in a theological, rather than in a legal, or racial, sense. What is known of the character of the church at Rome in the closing years of the first century indicates that it was much more in accord with the tradition of the Jerusalem church than in line with Paul's beliefs.[18]

In Paul's letter to the Philippians which was written while he was a prisoner in Rome, expecting death at any moment, there are clear indications that many in the Roman church were hostile to him and to his interpretation of the gospel. Probably the disagreements were the same as those between Paul and the Jerusalem authorities which had caused such trouble and which had embarrassed Peter in Antioch. If these differences did exist in Rome, there was need for Paul to set forth in the clearest, most comprehensive and most convincing way possible a full statement of his gospel and to send it on ahead to prepare the way for his arrival in Rome.

On first reading, chapter 16 of this letter creates the impression that Paul had many old friends in Rome. But chapter 16 may be a fragment of another letter that became attached to the letter to Rome. The last verse of chapter 15 sounds like the ending of the letter. The tone of 16:17-20 is more appropriate to a letter addressed to a church in which Paul had already been at work. The character and number of the greetings in chapter 16 seem to suggest a church with which Paul had a close acquaintance. There is also evidence that the letter to the Romans circulated among the churches in several different forms.[17] This is quite understandable since such a comprehensive statement of the gospel would be recognized as valuable and useful wherever there were Christians with genuine discernment.

Paul's letter to the Romans begins with a brief greeting (1:1-7) in which he identifies himself as an apostle and slave of Christ. He inserts a brief introductory statement of his gospel. Good news of *God,* good news in fulfillment of the promises of the Scriptures, good news of the Son of Man and Son of God through whom new life is open to all people. Repeatedly he emphasizes how eager he has been for some time to visit the Roman church and share with its members his knowledge of the gospel (vv. 8-15). Paul then launches quickly into his major theme: the power of God in Jesus to bring men truly alive when they respond in faith (vv. 16-17). But the revelation of new life in Christ, which is the *joy* of believers is at the same time a revelation of how universally all persons, good and bad alike, religious and irreligious, are alienated from God and are missing their true life (1:18—3:20). Even the Jew with his Scriptures and his obedience to the Law shares in this alienation. The theme of the "new righteousness of faith" returns (in 3:21) to emphasize how Christ's death frees men and women from their dead past (3:25). What God's promise foreshadowed in Abraham is fulfilled on behalf of all people in the death and resurrection of Jesus (Rom. 4).

Romans 5—8 traces the dimensions of the revolutionary change which the new righteousness makes in human life. All events take on new significance when men and women are *at peace with God* and their world is ruled by God's love. They begin a journey from the world of sin and death (which they now recognize for what it is) to a world of light and life. The old self that was under the tyranny of sin dies with Christ and rises with him into the new age inaugurated by his resurrection (Rom. 6).

There is a new obedience: no longer a slavish obedience under the law, but the free obedience which is made possible by grace. Freedom *from* the law does not mean law*less*ness but that law comes to have its proper function—no longer a way of salvation but rather a guide for those whom faith has set free *for* obedience (Rom. 7). We need such guidance on our way out of the old era into the new—a journey that takes a lifetime. The climax of the Christian's liberation is in his freedom from judgment and from death (Rom. 8). The whole creation is in travail in its longing to escape the deadly perversions of its life and to achieve the victory of imperishable life assured in Jesus Christ, as found in Romans 5 and 6.

Romans 9 through 11 takes up the problem of the Jew who for centuries cherished the promise of such a victory but seems now to be shut out from it by his rejection of the gospel. The rejection, however, is only temporary and has actually served God's purpose. It has sent the gospel more rapidly to the Gentile world (Rom. 9—11). Eventually Jew and Gentile will share together in the fulfillment of God's purpose.

Finally Paul outlines in Romans 12—15 the full character of the life which is the fruit of faith, showing how Christians should act and how they should respond to particular problems when once they have committed themselves decisively to the new age.

A NOBLE RELIGION AND A HIGH MORALITY MIGHT BE THE VERY
MEANS WHEREBY MEN AND WOMEN WOULD ATTEMPT TO JUS-
TIFY THEMSELVES AND PROTECT THEMSELVES AGAINST GOD'S
MORE RADICAL CLAIM ON THEM—THAT THEY SHOULD PLACE
THEMSELVES AT HIS DISPOSAL FOR A NEW VENTURE INTO THE
FUTURE. [33]

DARE WE GO BEYOND RELIGION TO FAITH? [35]

AS A CHRISTIAN, PAUL CAME TO SEE
THAT PEOPLE'S MOST STUBBORN RESISTANCE TO GOD WAS ROOTED
IN A SELF-CONFIDENCE CONCERNING THEIR PRESENT RELIGIOUS
AND MORAL SUPERIORITY. [33]

WE ARE FACED WITH THIS QUESTION:
DO WE STAND WITH PAUL,
OR WITH SOME WATERED DOWN VERSION
OF CHRISTIANITY? [35]

TO OUR DYING DAY TO STAND BE-
FORE GOD IS TO STAND WITH THE
PUBLICAN, AND PRAY, "GOD, BE
MERCIFUL TO ME A SINNER." [51]

[WHEN] TRUTH IS CHANGED INTO
FALSEHOOD, HUMAN RELATIONS ARE REDUCED TO A STATE OF
ANARCHY. [53]

chapter II
BEYOND RELIGION

We must be prepared to hear from Paul things which may cause us to question our own current religious ideas and practices. For instance, Paul calls himself the 'servant' or 'slave' of Jesus Christ. The word he uses here has had a long and significant history in the prophetic faith. In the Old Testament, it is customary for the man or woman who was used by God to carry forward His purpose in Israel to be called the 'servant' or 'slave' of God. (The same term was used in the ancient East for the man who stood next to the king, the prime minister. He was known as the *slave* of the king because his will was bound unconditionally to the king's will, and he was the primary agent for implementing or carrying out that will).

The prophet, who speaks in Isaiah 40 through 66, develops most fully this concept of 'slave of

God.' God needs such a slave, bound to him in the midst of history, if he is to get on with his saving purpose for all mankind. Israel is his chosen slave. To Israel he has entrusted the word which has the power to transform the earth from a desert into a fruitful garden (Isa. 55:10-13). The slave of God must withstand the enmity and hatred of a world which resists God. In faithfulness to God's word he must be prepared to suffer and die (Isa. 50 and 53). But such a death becomes the very means by which God breaks the resistance of men and women to his purpose and binds them to himself.

For Paul the 'Word,' by means of which God has now begun the decisive transformation of the world, is 'Jesus Christ.' To be a Christian is to be bound to that 'word.' But, since the 'word' is Christ, Paul can say that he is crucified with Christ so that it is no longer he who lives but Christ who lives in and through him. (Gal. 2: 20). He is not describing some inner mystical experience but an awakening and reproducing in himself of the same life and mission which was present in Jesus.

Paul's conversion was not from irreligion to religion, or from unbelief to belief, or from immorality to morality, but from a deeply earnest form of religion to become the slave of Christ.

We do well to remember that the Jewish religion of the first century was the purest and noblest religion in the ancient world, and that its Pharisaic sect—to which Paul belonged—represented its most progressive, earnest and intelligent development. The worship in the synagogue, with good reason, attracted many Gentiles. Prior to his conversion, Paul valued this whole order so highly that he was prepared to use violence to protect it when he saw it threatened by the Christian movement. We must ask what it was in his confrontation with Jesus Christ that made him leave it all behind. He recognized in Jesus the final and decisive manifestation of that transforming word of God which through the centuries had ever called a people into its service in order to carry forward God's saving purpose. A noble religion and high morality were not enough. In fact, a noble religion and high morality might be the very means whereby men and women would attempt to justify themselves and protect themselves against God's more radical claim on them—that they should yield themselves unconditionally to the will and purpose of God and place themselves at his disposal for a new venture into the future.

As a Christian, Paul came to see that man's most stubborn resistance to God was rooted in a self-confidence concerning his present religious and moral superiority. The tragedy of his fellow-countrymen was that this self-confidence was blinding them to how God was working in Jesus to break open the way for his saving purpose to move out from Israel into the whole world.

What we call Christianity is constantly in danger of losing its unique character and calling as the servant of God's transforming word in the midst of the life of mankind. When that happens it becomes merely a superior form of religion and virtue. We should make the test of comparing ourselves with pre-Christian Paul. Are we as earnest about our religion as he was, as determined to meet all its requirements, as well-versed in its Scriptures and its traditions, as zealous for its survival? As far as religious devotion and practice are concerned Paul was already far beyond most of us. Yet he came to recognize that all he had achieved was as nothing in comparison with a faith in which one's life was caught up into the great unfolding purpose of God for the redemption of the world (Phil. 3:7-11).

To be 'religious' is one thing: to be the slave of Christ, the slave of God, is quite another; and the two should not be confused! Only the slave of Christ enters with him into the new age that is dawning. Unless we understand this we have no chance of understanding what Paul means when he speaks of the 'righteousness of God' and 'justification by faith.' Yet this is the very problem of much of our American Christianity: it has become no more than a form of respectable, or, perhaps even, superior religion and morality in which the believers have no thought whatsoever of being 'slaves of Christ,' of putting themselves at God's disposal for any great and revolutionary transformation of the world's life or their own. We are faced with this question: Do we stand with Paul, or with some contemporary watered-down version of Christianity? Our decision could be costly. Dare we go beyond religion to faith?

THE RIGHTEOUSNESS OF GOD

No one could be expected to know without investigation what Paul means by the "righteousness of God." Grammatically the phrase could mean either a righteousness which is God's character, or a righteousness which has its origin in God and comes from him to us. Yet another meaning is suggested by the use of the word in Second Isaiah[18] and in Psalms[19] where it denotes an order which will prevail in human life throughout the world when all nations have been brought under the rule of God. This meaning is very close to what Jesus called "the kingdom of

God." All three meanings may, at times, be present in Paul's use of 'righteousness,' but sometimes one meaning is more prominent than the others.

The background of Paul's choice of this phrase, the 'righteousness of God,' to describe the reality of the Christian's life in God stems from his preconversion, life-long attempt to establish his own righteousness before God by a scrupulously careful obedience to God's law. Before Paul's Damascus-road experience the law was his way of salvation—the means by which he and all men might reach the fulfillment of their destiny. In spite of the law's complexity, it was a simple religious formula—obey the code and you may count on God's favor. Today many men mistakenly think they are Christian when they obey a simple code which they have extracted from the New Testament.

As a Christian, Paul now realized that obedience to the code led only to self-righteousness—a justification of one's self before God, that closed the mind to any new venture of faith to which God might be challenging his people. An Israel blinded by such self-righteousness had shown no openness either to John the Baptist or to the mission of Jesus. God had spoken his new word through John and through Jesus, yet they had not heard, and righteous Paul had not heard. But on the Damascus road Paul's ears were opened to hear.

In II Corinthians 12, Paul describes his experience of a vision of God, and in Galatians 1:16 (RSV note) he tells of God's revealing his Son, not just to him, but *in* him. (Most translations say 'to him' but the original Greek says 'in him.') A totally new possibility of life was opened to him and, in Romans, Paul calls this the "righteousness of God"—in contrast to his own self-achieved righteousness. It is not just a new quality of life, nor a new form of religion, but a new era in human existence, grounded in a new relationship with God and made possible for all through the life, death, and resurrection of Jesus Christ. It is offered to them as a free gift.

Paul begins his presentation in Romans 1:16 by saying that *he is "not ashamed of the gospel"* which proclaims the dawning of this new era for mankind. He was well aware that what he had to say might sound ridiculous to some people. The gospel does not consist of simple obvious truths. Many of its assertions, when first heard, may sound like nonsense—and no one likes to be caught talking nonsense. Our familiarity with these assertions often conceals from us how fantastic they really are: a young Jew from Nazareth who went about teaching and healing for a short time, then was executed as a criminal, was —in his person—the turning-point in all human history! By his death he overcame the power of evil that disrupts the world's life and by his resurrection he assured men of a life that is imperishable! God himself has been among men in this young Jew and continues to be present in him wherever he is remembered! In Paul's day such statements were real stumbling blocks to Jews and were nonsense to Greeks (I Cor. 1:23). And we ought not to be surprised when, in our day, intelligent people find them difficult to understand. Also, it may explain why, in contrast to Paul, we have at times had feelings of shame or embarrassment about the gospel. We have been reluctant to use language which, we vaguely realized, would sound unreasonable. Such language only becomes reasonable from within the new world of faith. Only when for us as for Paul it expresses our own directly personal faith—not just what we have heard from someone else, or even from the Scriptures—but what we know for ourselves, are we able to speak of the gospel with confidence and without embarrassment.

When Paul goes on to describe the gospel as "the power of God for salvation to everyone who has faith" he may well be thinking of the contrast between his present *faith* and his past *religion*. The dominant spirit of his religion before his confrontation with Christ had been defensiveness. He and his colleagues had been defending a rich religious heritage. But the dominant spirit of the Christian movement from its very beginning had been an aggressiveness. It was not indifferent to the past. It was rooted in the Israel of the Old Testament. But it was open to the action of God in creating new possibilities of life, breaking open new doors into the future. In the old religion God had been worshipped reverently—at a distance. In the new faith God was with man, breathtakingly close, the pivot of his existence, making all things new and different. There was a constant expectation of His saving action.

We frequently make the mistake of thinking of God's power and action in physical, external terms. For Paul the point in human history where God had acted most powerfully is a point where, to us, God might seem to have been most completely absent or powerless—the cross with Jesus Christ on it, betrayed by a friend, condemned by his enemies. God's action is a hidden action, visible to us only where faith has laid our whole being open to what is being done for us on the Cross.

The word 'salvation' has frequently been misunderstood and misused and needs interpretation. It was once monopolized by revivalistic religion and made to refer solely to the experience in which an unbeliever is converted. According to this view, 'saved' and 'converted' are interchangeable terms and the scope of salvation is confined narrowly to this initial experience of individuals. But for Paul salvation has a much larger meaning. It compasses the entire Christian life—from one's first response to God's call in the gospel through all the years of pilgrimage until beyond death the believer is at one with the Lord. Paul can say, "For salvation is nearer to us now than when we first believed" (Rom. 13: 11). It is both a present experience and a future hope. But it reaches far beyond the individual. The world has to be saved! The whole creation groans in travail waiting to see its transformation, when mankind shall have reached its destined goal as sons of God (Rom. 8:22). People in their sin and blindness poison not only themselves but also, as we now begin to recognize, their whole environment. Salvation, therefore, is not just the rescuing of *individuals* from an evil world, but rather a rescuing of individuals, communities, and the environment, from destructive forces which make them something less than

God's good creation. The primary agent to bring about this rescue is the gospel.

We may find it puzzling when Paul says that salvation is sent "to the Jew first and also to the Greek." By "Greek" he means all the Gentiles. But does he mean that the Jew has a special standing and takes precedence over all other men in relation to God, that the Jew has a special "in" with God that puts everyone else in second place? Elsewhere Paul says that in Christ the wall between Jew and Gentile has been broken down and both are one in him (I. Cor. 12:13, Gal. 3: 28). (See Chapter V on the relation between Jew and Christian.) But Paul was deeply aware of the continuity between Israel and the Christian church. The salvation in which he rejoiced was already promised and foreshadowed in the history of his people as recorded in the Scriptures (Rom. 1:2, 3:20). It burst forth in the mission of Jesus which was almost exclusively a mission to Jews. Not until later did it reach out in any large way to the Gentiles. In this sense the Jew had priority, and came first, but this priority laid upon him a greater responsibility.

We are more ready now perhaps to wrestle with that most knotty and most crucial verse 17 of Romans 1 which speaks of "the righteousness of God revealed through faith for faith," and which in support of this statement, paraphrases Habakkuk 2:4, "He who through faith is righteous shall live." What makes this web of words difficult to understand is that Paul expects us to know that he is talking about Jesus Christ, though he does not name him. The gospel of which he is speaking is the gospel of Christ crucified and risen. Christ is the one through whom God acts with power. The righteousness of God is revealed in Christ as a life of God with man and of mankind with God which brings human life to its true fulfillment. The word "faith" is used four times in verses 16 and 17 without any mention of its object. But the object is understood. Faith is the name for the new relationship between God and man when man is bound to Christ and lives henceforward in intimate, personal relation with him.

The righteousness of God can best be understood as the new age that is dawning or being revealed in Jesus Christ. Jesus himself proclaimed its coming. In Galilee he declared that it was at hand and called on his people to repent—that is —to turn round to begin life in the new age (Mark 1:15). When he freed men and women from the tyranny of evil forces, he said that their liberation was a sign of the presence of the Kingdom (Matt. 12:28). The words of his teaching were seeds of truth planted in the mind to grow *hiddenly* and to blossom in their own good time, bringing forth this new age (Mark 4:26-28).

The Kingdom was already present wherever men and women were open to receive it, and this openness to God lent to their faith power to move mountains (Matt. 17:20). Yet this presence was only the herald of the dawn. Jesus urged his disciples to pray for the coming of the kingdom when God's will would be done on earth as it is in heaven. Their first taste of its joy and power should make them hunger and thirst for its greater coming (Matt. 5:6). Here we note that in Matthew 5:20 Jesus calls the life of the kingdom righteousness, a righteousness that goes far beyond the righteousness of the scribes and Pharisees.

The new age first of all vindicates God's righteous purpose for his world and for humanity. The evil and misfortune which darken life for so many have caused them to ask in every generation, "Is God righteous?" The psalmist asked, "Why do the wicked prosper?" (Psalm 73) And the discouraged Judeans, who had seen Jerusalem destroyed complained that God had not dealt justly with them (Isa. 40:27). Every fresh disaster stirs the question anew, "Why do human beings have to suffer?" But in Jesus Christ God is revealed, not as inflicting evil on a helpless world, but as himself suffering with man under the burden and pain of the world's evil, yet making his righteous and gracious purpose triumph for man's blessing—in spite of, and even in the midst of, evil. The Cross reveals a righteous God at work redeeming a world that resists him in its unrighteousness, a world that cannot rob him of his ultimate triumph.

Again, 'righteousness' describes the character of life in the new age in all its relationships. In Israel belief in God and belief in a world in which justice and mercy prevail are inseparable. The injustice and cruelty of man are never accepted as a natural and inevitable element in human life but are understood as man's rejection of his destiny and perversion of God's good creation. But so pervasive are they in the life of the world that they can be overcome only by a divine invasion, a coming of God into the life of man to take over the place of rule that is being denied him. Thus the coming of God is the coming of God's kingdom, not just an inner experience for individuals but the establishment of a new order of life and a new quality in human relationships, for which one name is 'righteousness' and another is 'love.'

In a third sense the righteousness of God is a

righteousness *from* God which is his gift in Jesus Christ to those who in faith are open to receive it. It is nothing other than the life which Jesus himself lived and which he invited others to share with him. His selflessness, his humility, his understanding of others, his breadth of vision, his ability to speak the word men needed to hear, were all the consequence of his complete openness to God, described sometimes as the indwelling of the Spirit in him, sometimes as his "oneness with the Father." His life was a life in God, before God, in unbroken fellowship with God, empowered by God. But it was his life that *it might eventually become the life of all men.*

Jesus was uniquely the Son of God, not in lonely isolation, but that *all of us,* through him, might become children of God. The life he lived, he lived in the power of the Spirit. The same Spirit was soon to be poured out upon his disciples to empower them to live the life of the new age.

No word can better describe the life of Jesus, which was to be the life of the new age, than humanity. The presence of God with man in Jesus did not make him some special kind of religious man. It simply made him human, truly human, with no *speck* or *iota* of inhumanity left in him. The new righteousness was the triumph of humanity over *in*humanity. The fruit of God's coming was that at last in Jesus man became the creature reflecting God's nature (Gen. 1:26) that he was created to be.

This new humanity was revealed in Jesus Christ *through faith for faith.* Faith is a key word for Paul. He uses it over and over here to emphasize that *there is no door or way of access into the life of the new age—except Jesus Christ.* What is opposite to faith is works: the works of the law, obedience to the code by which in every age men have tried to achieve a merit, a standing with God, a righteousness of their own. Paul had abundant experience of that himself. He had once considered himself quite a success in that endeavor. He could boast of the precision and exactitude with which he obeyed the law. But the righteousness revealed in Jesus Christ made the righteousness Paul had achieved by 'law' appear not just inadequate but an act of folly, a product of his own blindness. Not until faith was born in him in confrontation with Jesus Christ, were his eyes opened to see the colossal difference between man-made righteousness and God-made humanity. Only faith had eyes to recognize the dawning of a new world in Christ. It dawned through faith and for the man of faith.

The quotation from Habakkuk 2:4 caps the

argument: "He who through faith is righteous shall live." This is not exactly what Habakkuk wrote. The Hebrew is better translated: "The righteous shall live by his faithfulness," in which *faithfulness* to God and his will is seen to be what enables men to survive in a time of upheaval. Paul adapts the text to his own purpose with the assistance of the Greek translation.[20]

"He who through faith is righteous," now becomes not just any man who is faithful to God but any man who is bound to Jesus Christ by faith and laid open to God through him so that he shares with Christ the righteousness of the new age and in it is truly alive both in time and eternity.

THE UNRIGHTEOUSNESS OF MAN

If righteousness (true humanity) is possible only through faith in Jesus Christ, everything which men have achieved apart from him and by their own endeavors is something *less than* and *other than* their true humanity. Verses 17 and 18 of the first chapter of Romans must be held closely together, not separated as though there were two revelations, one of the new age of righteousness and the other of God's wrath against all ungodliness and wickedness of men. The theme of Romans 1:18 through 3:20 is the universality of human sin—that all men, religious and irreligious, believers and unbelievers, moral and immoral, must confess themselves sinners before God. But this is not an obvious truth to be observed merely by examining the characters of men. General observation is more likely to convince us, as indeed most persons are convinced, that mankind divides naturally into two categories, the good and the bad, the righteous and the wicked, the believers and the unbelievers, the godly and the ungodly.

If we examine ourselves we shall find that we are constantly assigning people to the one category or the other, the good or the bad. Invariably we assign ourselves to the more enlightened, virtuous, godly category. We reserve the wrath of God for the wicked and ungodly. But Paul does not agree, nor does Jesus, as we shall see.

This should warn us that here is one point where the Christian gospel breaks across our customary way of thinking, contradicting it. When we stand before God, really in his presence, in the light that shines from the face of Jesus Christ, all our distinctions of good and bad, righteous and wicked, godly and ungodly, are made relative, our self-confidence is shaken, and all of us are *revealed* to ourselves as sinners against God, as enemies in some degree of his purpose for humanity. Here then we discover our most fatal blindness about ourselves which alienates us from God and disrupts our relationships with our fellowmen.

At this point the Jesus of the Gospels and the Paul of the Letters are at one and agree, though they express themselves very differently. The spiritual paralysis which Jesus detected in Pharisees was rooted in their self-righteousness. Refraining from obvious sins and performing deeds of merit they blinded themselves (Luke 18:11, 12) to their less obvious but more serious sins and nurtured a contempt for many of their fellowmen. Jesus' estimate of mankind is evident in the parable which he addressed to a Pharisee (Luke 7:41-42). There are only two categories, those who owe God a greater debt and those who owe a lesser debt. Both are bankrupt and are dependent wholly on God's mercy since they have no way in which to settle the debt.

There are no righteous men. A failure to know this makes Pharisees of all of us. Our confidence in our own righteousness is based upon false data, a lie that is the consequence of comparing ourselves with others instead of facing the truth about ourselves as it appears when we stand before God. Jesus found this pride and self-confidence of the religious man to be a far greater obstacle to God than the more obvious sins that are readily pronounced wicked and cause persons to be banned from the society of the "virtuous and godly."

Perhaps we can now understand why the revelation of God's righteousness in Jesus Christ was at the same time the revelation of the universality of human sin for Paul. To be confronted by Jesus Christ and to have one's eyes opened by faith to the Life that was present in him was to know two things at once: God's offer in Christ of the really human life for which we were created and God's rejection of the inhuman life to which, in varying degrees, we have let ourselves become committed. His offer of life reveals his love for us. His rejection of us as we are reveals his wrath against all that obstructs his purpose for us and his world.

What Paul calls "the wrath of God" is frequently misunderstood. The phrase conjures up a picture of a God who is sometimes loving and sometimes angry. What is described in Scripture as God's wrath or God's judgment expresses our painful awareness of God's unswerving opposition to all that resists his gracious and loving purpose for his world. God's love, resisted, is felt as wrath. Francis Thompson in his poem, *The Hound of Heaven,* has given graphic expression to this truth. Man, fleeing God in terror, sees only hostile forces in his world; but, once captured by God's love, he finds his whole world transformed. God would not be God and his love for man would be an empty sentiment if he did not hate and reject everything that makes man less than human. God's love and God's wrath are therefore two ways of experiencing the same reality in God. We see this plainly in words of Jesus which express the love of God. A parable such as that of the Pharisee and the Publican has in it both divine acceptance and divine rejection but in both responses God is in search of man.

The universality of sin does not mean the universality of badness, that all people from their first to their last breath are evil. In the past, Paul has sometimes been thought to have had a very bleak and dismal view of all men *except* Christians. How wrong this is becomes evident, first of all, from the fact that, for Paul, *all* (including himself and all Christians) *are sinners.* There are no exceptions. To our dying day, to stand before God is to stand with the publican and pray, "God, be merciful to me, a sinner" (Lk. 18:13).

Sin is anything and everything in us that resists God's purpose for us and for his world. Sin is our alienation from God. Sin is our imprisonment in a self, possibly a very well-behaved and earnestly religious self—but one not really open either toward God or toward our fellow men.

To Jesus, sin was a sickness of the self that left it broken, and unready for life. The word sin has come to be surrounded by so many false meanings that we may have to use some other terms to grasp the reality of it. The language of the existentialist theologians is helpful when they speak of an inauthentic self in contrast to an authentic self. Everyone has the experience of being *alienated* from his true self, of reaching out toward a self not yet realized. The fully authentic self is at the end of the journey. In calling this universal inauthenticity or alienation, *sin,* the Christian faith lays responsibility on every man for what he is, and sees beneath man's *alienation* from himself a separation or alienation from God. Genesis 3 still takes us to the root of the problem when it traces man's tragic distortion of his world, not to some wicked impulse, but to *the desire for a freedom without limits,* in short, to *the drive of the self to be its own sovereign ruler.*

In Romans 1:18-32 Paul's focus is on the pagan world of his time. He is not intending to present a balanced picture of Graeco-Roman society, evaluating its virtues and its vices. The classical scholar might object that he has catalogued all the vices which admittedly were present, but has left out all the brighter aspects of that society. For Paul it is sufficient that in the world at large people have lost their way and are missing their destiny. It is not that they have been left without any knowledge of the will of God. They have had their philosophers and religious teachers who have discerned a presence of the divine and standards of right and wrong. But such knowledge has been corrupted by sin and blindness, making human beings proud of their supposed wisdom while they are actually prisoners of folly. Truth has been changed into falsehood and the worship of God into a worship of idols, reducing human relations to a state of anarchy.

In Romans 2 Paul turns sharply upon the religious and moral man. He may have in mind a Jewish Christian, or a Gentile who was attached to the synagogue before he became a Christian. It is someone who would agree with his attack on Gentile vices. In verse 17 Paul speaks directly to his fellow Jews who are only too sure that Gentile sinners deserve the wrath of God. They willingly sit in judgment on them, assuming that they, themselves—as members of an earnestly religious community—are free from judgment. They are not sinners like the Gentiles; in pronouncing such favorable judgment on themselves they have become self-righteous like the Pharisees! And self-righteousness is actually the most stubborn form of alienation from God. They are blind to the fact that as members of their communities they share responsibility for the corruptions which they condemn in their neighbors. They think that the mercy and kindness of God which they claim for themselves frees them from any fear of God's judgment upon their sins (2: 4). But there is to be a day of judgment for all mankind when God will reward each person according to his or her deeds. In that day of judgment some pagan Gentiles may fare better than the Jews or the Christians who pride themselves on their knowledge of God's law. The Gentiles who in their consciences have a knowledge of right and obey their consciences take precedence over the Jew or the Christian who knows the law but does not obey it. It is not the hearers but rather the doers of the law who are righteous before God (Romans 2:13).

This last sentence presents us with a problem. In verse 13 Paul seems to speak of a justification by obedience to the law, yet elsewhere he insists that justification is by faith alone. The primary point here is that God judges or measures us not by our words—or our profession of faith—but by our deeds. No mere profession of faith justifies unless it bears fruit in the obedience of faith—the translation of faith into action. (Verse 16 should be read directly after verse 13. It has been misplaced somehow as the text was copied.)

In Romans 2:17-29 and 3, Paul anticipates the presence in the Roman church of Jewish Christians who belonged to the faction that for some years has been most hostile to his interpretation of the gospel. Probably this accounts for the sharpness of his tone at this point in what on the whole is a rather conciliatory, and noncontroversial presentation of the gospel. For these Judaizers the Christian church was a Jewish sect. To be members of it Gentiles had not only to have faith in Jesus as the Christ, but had also to take upon themselves the distinctive marks of the Jew—circumcision and the restrictions of kosher food laws. The law of Judaism and the gospel of Jesus *together* formed the basis of their Christianity. As a consequence they carried over into the Christian Church a Pharisaic form of religion in their zeal for the Jewish law and their confidence in an ability to instruct others in the ways of God (Romans 2:18-21a). They were specially lacking in humility and blind to their own failings and deficiencies. Paul therefore defines for them the true Jew who is to be known, not by any outward marks, but by the inward submission of the heart and life to God (2:27-29).

In Romans 3:1-8 Paul continues to argue with his fellow Jews in Rome. He can imagine what their objections will be to what he has been saying for he has heard it all before: in bringing all men, Jew and Gentile alike, under the judgment of God, he has made it seem that there is no advantage in being an Israelite, a member of the historic people of God. (We would say, ". . . in being a Christian, a member of the church of God.") Paul seems to them to have reduced Gentile and Jew to the same level. (We would say, destroyed the distinction between Christian and non-Christian. If all are sinners under God's judgment, what advantage is there in being a member of the Church?) Paul's answer is that the Jew (we would say the Christian) is not to pride himself upon his moral and spiritual superiority but upon the fact that he has been entrusted with the oracles of God—the Scriptures in which God makes himself known to men and reveals to them his purpose for them and for his world. The sacred calling of the Jew (and of the Christian) is to be the custodian of the treasure beyond all other treasures, the knowledge of God which alone makes a truly human life possible. The true Jew is the slave of God's word who lives to make it known. That some Jews (and Christians) have been and are unfaithful does not negate the greatness of Israel's (or the church's) calling. God has always had to work through a remnant and the unfaithfulness of men makes the faithfulness of God appear all the brighter.

The thought of Romans 3:5-8 is obscure until set against the background of Paul's assertions in Romans 9 through 11. The rejection of the gospel by the Jews has actually been made by God to serve his glory by hastening the mission to the Gentiles. That God uses even the unfaithfulness of men to forward his purpose is a familiar teaching of Paul. But now he hears his opponents twisting his words and trying to argue that if men's sin serves God's glory, they should not be condemned for it. Rather they should be encouraged to sin more vigorously so that God may have the greater glory! Paul knows that this is the doctrine slanderously attributed to him by some men (3:8).

Romans 3:9-20 sums up the whole discussion of the universality of sin, supporting and buttressing the argument with a series of quotations from the Old Testament which would have strong authority for the Jewish mind. Obedience to the law was long the basis of Paul's confidence in his relationship with God and in the 20th century it still remains the basis of confidence for some Christians. But now Paul knows from his own experience that there is no salvation, no lasting peace with God, no new life, by way of the Law. On that road one always ends up in a barren self-righteousness. The law was never meant to be a way of salvation but only a spelling out of what God expects of those who respond to him in faith. Faith must come first, before there can be *true* obedience.

THE GIFT OF JUSTIFICATION

In verses 21-30 Paul picks up again the theme of 'righteousness through faith' (which he first announced in 1:16, 17), but now the alternate term, 'justification by faith,' becomes central. It introduces a new element, since the word 'justify' carries a legal background. It means, in some contexts, God's acceptance of the sinner as righteous in spite of the fact that in some degree he continues to be a sinner. One can readily understand that such a doctrine was open not only to misunderstanding, but also to misuse. What is this righteousness which God confers on sinners as a free gift if they have faith in Jesus Christ? Is this not too easy a way into God's favor and an encouragement to ignore the claims of God's law? Such objections could come only from those who had never come face to face with Jesus Christ or experienced the claims of his person upon them.

To respond to him in faith is to be received, in spite of one's unworthiness, into a share in his life.

The good news of the gospel is that our sin and unworthiness do not need to shut us out forever from the presence of God. We do not have to wait until we have made ourselves worthy by obedience. That endeavor is futile, for no man can ever be worthy before God. What God came seeking in Jesus was not the worthy or the righteous. Those who esteemed themselves worthy and righteous were blind to God's presence in Jesus and hostile to him. His search was for persons who, knowing their unworthiness, would respond to him with their whole being, that is, with faith. Where he found such faith he bestowed a new life, a life that in its righteousness was far beyond what any man could attain by his own most earnest efforts. We must not miss Paul's comment, however, in verse 21, that although *this new righteousness far transcends the life that he knew under the law,* it is the *fulfillment of the hopes long ago expressed in the Law and the Prophets, the Scriptures of Israel* (cf. Matt. 5: 20). Old Testament men of vision saw the new age from afar.

A new note is sounded in verse 25 which will require much fuller consideration later. Thus far Paul has said only that the righteousness and wrath of God are revealed. In interpreting his words we had to understand that both are revealed in *Jesus Christ*. Now we learn that they are revealed supremely in the cross of Jesus Christ. This is a mystery. How can a young Galilean Jew who was executed in Jerusalem as though he were a criminal, by his death set men free from the tyranny of sin and reconcile them to God? Yet this is the very source and wellspring of the Christian's life. At the Cross he sees revealed the awesome gulf between an alienated humanity and God. In that gulf, bridging it and overcoming the alienation, is the figure of Jesus giving himself as a sacrifice for the sake of his fellow men. Faith in Jesus is no cheap way of access to God. The Jesus to whom faith responds is a Jesus who seals his bond of faithfulness to God with a cross. The love that in him becomes our life is crucified love. Therefore it is not possible for us to share his life in God unless we are ready to share his cross. His gift of life to us is, both for him and for us, a costly gift.

All persons alike have access to God in Jesus Christ. Whether Jew or Gentile, circumcised or uncircumcised, no man can be justified before God except by faith. At once Paul hears the Jewish objection to this pronouncement, namely that it overthrows the Torah, the Law. Law here may mean the law-code of Judaism or the Torah (one name for the Jewish Scriptures, our Old Testament). Jesus, too, we remember, had to defend himself against the accusation that *he* was doing away with the Scriptures (Matt. 5:17) and the charge against Stephen, when he was stoned to death, was that he "spoke against Moses" (Acts 6:11). (Moses being used here as another name for Scripture.) To speak against Scripture was to speak against God, a blasphemy punishable by death. We realize, therefore, that in Romans 3:31 Paul conjures up a dangerous charge against himself. Romans 4 is his answer.

ABRAHAM, THE MODEL OF FAITH

Paul anticipates that the Jewish Scriptures will have profound and strong authority in the Roman church—not only with Judaizing members, but with Gentiles who, in their pre-Christian days, had attended the synagogue. Therefore, any suspicion that his gospel contradicted the Scriptures would be fatal for the church. On the other hand, if he could show that his gospel was directly in line with the central tradition of the Scriptures, it would win acceptance.

All Jews counted themselves children of Abraham. He incarnated Israel's destiny. In the great credo of Deuteronomy 26:5-10 every Israelite was taught to identify himself with the faith and calling of Abraham. But what was the example of Abraham? He could not very well be a model of salvation by obedience to the law, for the Law was not given until centuries later in the time of Moses. Abraham was remembered above all because of his faith in God's promise. He was called to be the father of a people through whom God would bring great blessings to all mankind. The obstacles to the fulfillment of such a destiny were so forbidding as to make it seem impossible. Even when a son was born to Abraham and Sarah in their old age, hope of fulfillment of the promise seemed about to be crushed by God's demand that Abraham offer his only son as a sacrifice. Both in faith and in faithfulness Abraham was unswerving. God preserved his son from death as a seed that was to grow into the nation of Israel, and it was written of Abraham in Genesis 15:6, "He believed the Lord; and he reckoned it to him as righteousness." Abraham was the perfect model of faith.

Since, then, faith alone enables us to receive our share in Christ and in the life which is his gift to us, there is no room for a Jewish (or Christian) pride or boasting (3:27).

Then Paul quotes David, whom he takes to be

the author of Psalm 32, in support of this model of faith, as a witness that God's forgiveness is the way to a blessedness which cannot by any means be reserved for law-observing Jews alone. With this support Paul returns to Abraham with a rabbinic-sounding argument. He argues that since Abraham was not circumcised until after God reckoned his faith as righteousness, he was, first of all the father of the uncircumcised faithful, and only secondarily the father of circumcised and faithful Jews (Rom. 4:10-15). Abraham thus is "the father of us all" (v. 16), Gentile and Jew alike, and Paul's mission to the Gentiles is validated by the Scriptures.

Though Paul continues to write of Abraham in the remainder of the chapter, it is the Christian he really has in mind. Abraham's God (v. 17) is the God "who gives life to the dead and calls into existence the things that do not exist;" that is, he is the God who raised Jesus from the dead and who, through him, is bringing into being a new world that did not previously exist (vv. 24-25). Jesus died to free all men from their sins and rose again to open to them the life of justification—that is, a life lived daily in the presence and by the power of God—the fulfillment of the promise made to Abraham.

THE CROSS CAN BECOME THE DOORWAY
TO THE NEW WORLD FOR WHICH WE LONG. [82]

IT IS GOD WHO JUSTIFIES AND NOT
SOMETHING WE DO OR FEEL OR THINK OR
CHERISH. [67]

"CHRIST DIED FOR THE UNGODLY."
ROMANS 5:6 [67]

"PEACE WITH GOD THROUGH OUR LORD, JESUS CHRIST"
CAN NEVER BE SECURED AT A CUT-RATE PRICE. [75]

GOD TAKES A LIFETIME TO FASHION
HIS NEW WOMEN AND MEN AND MANY LIFETIMES TO FASHION
HIS NEW CREATION. [75]

FAITH IS OUR READINESS TO RECEIVE THE COSTLY
GIFT OF NEW LIFE THAT GOD OFFERS TO US IN
THE CRUCIFIED AND RISEN LORD. [67]

JESUS' MISSION WAS TO PREACH GOOD
NEWS TO THE POOR, TO PROCLAIM RELEASE TO THE CAPTIVES,
TO SET AT LIBERTY THE OPPRESSED. LUKE 4:18 [75]

chapter III

THE NEW AGE OF FAITH AND FREEDOM

THE FAITH THAT JUSTIFIES

The term 'justification by faith' takes on very different meanings according to our understanding of faith. To some people 'faith' is just an inner confidence in *an overshadowing Providence* that will make everything turn out all right. Its level rises and falls like water in a cistern. To others, faith is agreement with *some formulation of Christian doctrine.* Disagreement at any point would seem to them to cancel out their faith. To still others, faith is *commitment to a code of ideals* which they consider Christian or, more personally, *commitment in loyalty to Jesus.*

This divergence of meanings is perhaps encouraged by the fact that so often in the New Testament, and particularly in Paul's letters, the word 'faith' occurs by itself, without any clear indication what its object is. Jesus says to people, "Your faith has saved you." A man cries out to Jesus, "Lord, I believe." Paul writes ". . . since we are justified by faith, we have peace with God." In each of these instances the context defines the faith. The faith which Jesus commends is the glad and openhearted response to the word of forgiveness which *he* has spoken. The man who cried, "I believe," had the object of his faith directly before him in the divine presence and power he sensed in *Jesus*. So also with Paul. We must not separate Romans 4:24-25 from Romans 5:1. The faith of which he speaks in the latter is faith in him "who was put to death for our trespasses and raised for our justification."

Unless we let faith have its proper object [Jesus Christ in his birth, life, death, and resurrection], justification by faith is meaningless or misleading. In fact, we can turn it into a form of self-justification, the very thing Paul is trying to overcome.

It is so easy to think that we are justified before God by an inner confidence which we *feel* or by our willingness to accept the *right doctrines* or by some *religious experience* which we have had or by the high quality of the *ideals* we cherish—(each of these being understood as a form of faith) . It is necessary, therefore, to insist that it is *God* who justifies us and not something we do or feel or think or cherish. Moreover, our justification, which is our reconciliation with God (Rom. 5:10), is rooted and grounded in the death and resurrection of Jesus. We would avoid much misunderstanding if we spoke of being justified by a grace to which our faith is the response. 'Grace' is God's action on behalf of all men through the Cross and the Resurrection. Faith is our openness to God's action, our readiness to receive the costly gift of new life that God offers to us in the crucified and risen Lord. Faith has its true character and power only when it has this source. Everything else that men call faith is a poor, weak substitute without power to create either new men or a new world.

This unique definition of faith is validated again and again in Romans 5 and 6. In our helplessness and alienation we nevertheless can hope, since "Christ died for the ungodly" (Rom. 5:6). "While we were yet sinners Christ died for us" (5:8). "We are now justified by his blood" (5:9). The word 'blood' suggests the sacrificial character of Christ's death. "We were reconciled to God by the death of his Son" (5:10). "By one man's obedience [i.e., unto death] many will be made righteous" (5:19). Then in Romans 6, as Paul points up the meaning of baptism, he defines faith in Jesus Christ as a *dying with him in his death* and *a rising with him in his resurrection* into a new life and a new world (Rom. 6:3, 4). Faith is *union with Christ* (6:5)—not merely believing in him at a distance or believing something about him, but being one with him in an intimate, personal union—an openness to him in response to his openness to us. Therefore, just as Christ's death brought to an end the era of man's helplessness and enslavement, and his resurrection opened a new era in man's life with God, so the believer, in union with him, has died to the old world and to his old self, and finds himself in a new world in which the meaning of all his life's experiences is transformed by the change in his relationship with God.

THE TWO ERAS

We shall not understand Paul's thinking either here or elsewhere unless we grasp firmly the fact that Paul divides the life of mankind into two eras, life *before* and life *after* Christ's death and resurrection. We have a rough analogy of this in our calendar which divides all time into the years B.C. [Before Christ] and A.D. [Year of Our Lord]. But this is only superficial; it is simply an external, chronological, division. For Paul, the two eras denote two wholly different *orders* of life. In the one we are the prisoners of sin; our whole world is clouded and broken by our alienation, an estrangement not only from God but also from our fellow man and from ourselves. Death broods over us. In the other, we are the prisoners of God, set free from sin and death, and given a wholly new prospect of life in time *and* eternity by the reconciliation with God which creates new relationships with others and with ourselves.

The sharpness of Paul's definition of the division between these two worlds is undoubtedly colored by the sharpness of the break in his own life: his change [conversion] from a fanatical persecutor of Christians to an apostle of the Faith. The world of sin and death is by no means a world in which all people are evil and godless; it is the world in which Paul himself had tried with such earnestness to make himself right with God by keeping the law. It is more than the Jewish world: it is the entire world of broken persons who try to heal *themselves* with their various remedies, Jews by a scrupulous obedience to what they conceive to be God's will and Greeks by their attempt to make life conform to ideals of truth, beauty, and goodness. The pity of it all is that none of the remedies reaches deep enough. They merely improve the surface of life in a world that still remains the world of sin and death.

The new world that Paul saw dawning in Jesus Christ and in the Christian movement was not a reformation of the old, nor was the man of faith merely a reformed version of the religious man of Palestine or Greece. Christianity was not just a new and better religion, nor was Paul's conversion merely a transfer from Judaism to this new religion. What began in Jesus Christ was nothing less than a new creation—and to be 'in Christ' was to be, oneself, a new creature (II Cor. 5:17), participating in the powers of the new creation and in the breathtaking venture of the making of a new world.

The promise of a new world is a constant element in the Scriptures from beginning to end and belongs to the very essence of the biblical faith in God. In Genesis 1, the creation, still untainted and uncorrupted by evil, suggests a new creation yet to come when evil will be overcome (Isa. 51:6; 60:19, 20; Rev. 21:1). The Eden of Genesis 2 gives promise of a new Eden (Isa. 51:3; Rev. 22). Men and women of faith dream of a world in which there will be no more war, cruelty, want, or sorrow. Jeremiah saw that the covenant relation on which Israel's life had been built was an insufficient basis for the building of that new world. He foretold the coming of a time when God's law would be written in the hearts of all and their alienation from God and from themselves would cease (Jer. 31:33-34).

When Jesus proclaimed the nearness of the Kingdom, he was telling men that the long-desired new world was at their door, ready to break in upon them. They need wait for it no longer. They could begin now to know the joy and healing of its power. For the present, the coming would be a hidden coming, an inner transformation of the meaning of every experience in the world, not a full outward transformation of the world. True, it would begin to change the outward character of life, but the *final* outward transformation would have to wait until God brought history to a close. [Paul at first thought this final day to be very close at hand; he later saw it farther off.] Paul never doubted, however, that with the death and resurrection of Jesus, the new creation had begun and that the life of faith was life in the new age.

Today we tend in various ways to dissolve the vital and inescapable tension between Paul's two worlds. Individualistic piety has narrowed the horizon of faith to the inner life of persons; it has let the politicians take over the hope for a new world through their communist utopias and democratic "new societies"—which eventually add their own contributions to man's hopelessness. We categorize Christianity as one of the religions of man, perhaps the highest, and set it in series along with all the others. We emphasize the things these religions have in common, and ignore the central claim of the New Testament: to be announcing not the birth of a new religion but the birth of a new world and a new man.

In the name of Secularity we assert the oneness of all reality, and confine reality within the limits of what is historically observable, reducing God to a question mark and Paul's new creation to a questionable theory or speculative hypothesis! Talk of an old self or a new self seems nonsense: we are what we are, we say, and while we may undergo improvements, we have to content ourselves with the self we were born with. But if we insist on maintaining this negative attitude we have not only Paul against us but a whole panel of New Testament witnesses and, behind them, Jesus himself and the whole of the Old Testament.

It was this vital tension, between the familiar world and the promised world, that set Israel in motion for over a thousand years and made that tiny Palestinian nation the benefactor of millions yet unborn! It has been this same tension, over and over, that has made the Christian faith a revolutionary force in human society and in the lives of individuals. The worst mistake we can make is to fall into the common way of thinking: that regards the world of sin and death as the matter-of-fact, tangible reality and consigns the kingdom of God to the intangible realm of dreams and ideals. We fall into this trap and commit this error when we hold that man is *by nature* a sinner and the world is, *by nature,* evil. Sin and evil are *not* Reality but unreality; they are perversions of the world and mankind. We see the true nature of man in Jesus Christ. And the world which begins to be when life is made new by him is the Reality of God's good creation.

LIFE IN THE NEW AGE

When Paul begins to describe the life of the new age which has its origin in Jesus Christ, he speaks in personal terms. He testifies to what he knows and what he expects everyone who shares his faith to discover through their personal experience. He stands within the new age as he describes it:

"We have peace with God."

"We have obtained access to this grace in which we stand."

"We rejoice in our hope."

"God's love has been poured into our hearts."
"We rejoice in our sufferings."

There is a well-documented variation of Romans 5:1 which reads, "Let us have peace with God," but there are two strong arguments against this translation. First, justification is in itself reconciliation with God and therefore a making of peace, so that peace is not just a possibility, but an actuality; and second, all the other verbs in this paragraph are in the indicative, asserting what has already been achieved by Christ. However, these strong, confident assertions can be misunderstood—if justification is considered to be a doorway through which one passes directly *from* the old world of sin and alienation *into* a new world of immediate and complete peace and love. The language of Romans 6 encourages the same misunderstanding when Paul speaks of our old sinful self *dying* with Christ that we may rise with him into the new world of grace. The abruptness of Paul's own transition from the first order of life to the second, conditions his language. But he has no intention of encouraging anyone to think that in their conversion they have become free, once and for all, from their old self and from the world of sin and death. He has already laid great emphasis upon the universality of sin, a universality that by no means excuses the Christian (Rom. 1:18-3:20). Christians, to their dying day, know themselves to be sinners before God. Paul in Romans 7 lays bare the struggle that still goes on within himself, between the old self and the new. God takes a lifetime to fashion his new men and women and many lifetimes to fashion his new creation. The fulfillment is future and the Christian lives in hope of it, but his hope is nourished by what he experiences of God's new day in the present.

In recent years, 'Peace with God' has been offered to men in the religious marketplace at bargain rates. There have even been men who have become noted as specialists in providing the public with such peace, but the peace they offer is always a private and inner peace, unrelated to the problems of peace in the outer world. The possessors of this peace are never noted for their identification with the victims of injustice and exploitation, nor for their participation in movements to overcome the poverty, racial strife, or armed conflicts that make peace an impossibility for so many human beings. *"Peace with God through our Lord, Jesus Christ"* can never be secured at a cut-rate price. Jesus' mission was to preach good news *to the poor,* to proclaim release *to the captives,* to set at liberty *the oppressed* (Luke 4:18). Faith which binds us to him opens our hearts to the agony of our brothers who are despised, excluded, exploited, starved, trampled upon, injured, ill, ignored, forgotten.

The Christian is so deeply disturbed by human suffering that it seems impossible for him ever to be at peace. This is what makes the Christian's peace with God what Paul elsewhere calls a peace "that passes all understanding" (Phil. 4:7). He is at peace because he knows in Christ the power of God at work to overcome those forces of destructive conflict and needless suffering. The action of God in and through Jesus Christ is not just the creation of peace in the soul but the creation of peace between person and person and so eventually transforms all of life's relationships. Peace with God is inseparable from peace on earth.

"Access to this grace" is access to God. Grace is not something apart from God, but is God giving himself to us in his graciousness. It is "God with us" in his infinite readiness to help. We are no longer alone, dependent upon our own meager resources to meet our tasks and responsibilities. Our help does not have to come from some distant heaven. It is at hand, immediately. We can reach out and accept it. We can count on it to be present. Therefore we do not need to be afraid of any situation we may have to face. God's grace will always be sufficient. Paul, himself, had one personal problem that caused him continual distress, a thorn which he prayed again and again to have removed, but without success. But one day he heard, as a word from Christ, "My grace is sufficient for you, for my power is made perfect in [your] weakness" (II Cor. 12:7 ff). Human weakness ceases to be a reason for distress when it becomes the occasion for God to show us the strength of his supporting grace.

Having spoken of what the new relation with God through Christ means in the present, Paul now looks to the future and "rejoices in . . . hope of sharing the glory of God." The "glory" of God in Hebrew thought is the aura of his immediate presence, sometimes represented as a heavenly light or fire. The blinding light in which Christ appeared to Paul on the Damascus road suggests the glory of the divine presence. Paul's hope, therefore, is that the share he now has in part, that is, brokenly (I Cor. 13:12), in Jesus' life in God, will grow through faith until he sees God face to face and shares with Christ the glorious presence of the Father.

To be perfectly at one with God was for Paul the goal of life; and to have meaning for him life had to be the journey toward that goal. This was the destiny for which he and everyone had been created: to be in the likeness of God, to reflect the nature of God in personal relations. In his legalistic religion Paul had lost the prophetic vision of the goal; he had settled for a dull and plodding obedience to a legal code. But his encounter with Christ had been for him a fresh sighting of the goal of human destiny. It destroyed all complacency with his moral and spiritual attainments and set him in motion on an inner journey that would not be finished in his lifetime.

One should note how frequently Paul speaks of his joy. His life, in spite of the weight of his responsibilities and the severity of his sufferings, was a joyful existence. The secret of his joy was the reality of his inner journey toward the fulfillment of life itself in God. In Romans 5:3 Paul points out how his sufferings do not destroy his joy, but rather contribute to it. If we want to know a little of what he suffered we have only to read II Corinthians 11:23-29. We are likely to think of suffering and joy as mutually exclusive. It seems a bit sadistic or masochistic for any one to say that he "rejoices in suffering." But Paul's sufferings have a special character as penalties he endured in order to preach the gospel; through them he was conscious of sharing in the sufferings of Christ himself (Phil 3:10) . In them it was as though Christ himself were living his life anew. More than that, they help him on his way in his journey, building in him an endurance which strengthens his character and generates in him fresh hope of what he is yet to be.

The basis of assurance, however, is the living presence of God with man *now*, which is the immediate fruit of justification. To be justified is to be reconciled not with a God who remains at a distance, but with a God who chooses as his dwelling place the "humble and the contrite heart." The very essence of Jesus' mission in his lifetime, and as the risen Lord, was to share with others his own life in God. The secret of the fulfillment of humanity in him was the completeness with which he was indwelt by the presence and power of God. The name for that presence of God in us is "Holy Spirit."

We make a tragic mistake when we think of the Incarnation, God in man, as something that pertains exclusively to Jesus. The testimony of the whole New Testament is that Jesus was indwelt by God's Spirit so that *all* might be possessed by the same Spirit; that Jesus was uniquely Son of God that all might through him become sons of God. "God with us" means "God's spirit in us." God's spirit in us means the love of God "poured into our hearts" (Rom. 5:5). It turns us from ourselves to God and outward to our fellow man, transforming all our life's relationships.

CHRIST DIED FOR THE UNGODLY

The supreme example of the love of God was the willingness of Jesus to die for the sake of men who were unworthy of anything that he should do for them. The word "love" has so many meanings and connotations among us that it is not easy to grasp its New Testament meaning. Love is frequently no more than desire—for things or persons. In personal relations it rarely rises higher than mutuality: I will love you if you will respond in love to me—and a failure in the response brings the love to an end. But God's love in the New Testament is love that gives itself endlessly, and where it is not deserved. It has power to heal broken relations between God and man, or between individual and individual, because it gives itself without waiting for any response. It conquers hostility by loving even the enemy. What was more amazing in Jesus than his love for those who stood against him? (Exemplified in his last moments on the cross in his prayer for God's forgiveness of those who, in their ignorance and blindness, had crucified him.) In Jesus, a great compassion for humanity was let loose in the world. But its focal point was the

Cross. There, as Paul says, "Christ died for the ungodly."

Paul marvels at such love (Rom. 5:7). His words are confusing. "One will hardly die for a righteous man though perhaps for a good man one will dare even to die." Good man is not in the Greek text, only the word 'good,' so that a possible translation is, "Why, one will hardly die for a righteous man—though perhaps for a good cause one might dare to die." How amazing it is then that Jesus died for the sake of sinful humanity! But how is this true, that "Christ died for us?"

Many Christians would have to confess, in honesty, that the statement, "Christ died for us," leaves them cold. How can the tragic and unfortunate death of a Galilean Jew in Jerusalem, nearly twenty centuries ago, be a "dying for us sinners" today? It all depends upon who that Galilean was. What bound men to Jesus in those earliest days was the conviction that he was the bearer of truth and life, truth that was life, the one true life of man in God, in which a new age in the life of man was being born. Because that one true Life called all other lives into question (even the most virtuous and godly of them), he was rejected and crucified. He could have escaped his execution, but he would have escaped

III
81

also his destiny as the bearer of new life—a life which, by its nature, is God's judgment upon all that men called life and at the same time God's loving invasion of the world that resists him. Jesus went to his cross recognizing in agony that it was the necessary climax and fulfillment of his mission and of his obedience to God.

The Cross exposes to us how deep-rooted and stubborn is our human resistance to God, and how powerful and destructive our enmity and alienation can be—even while we are congratulating ourselves upon being the friends of God. When we really know ourselves, we know we are no better than Peter, perhaps no better than pre-Christian Paul or the disciple Judas. Yet, Christ died that we might one day find our alienation overcome and ourselves launched on the journey toward the true goal of our existence. The Christ of the Cross reveals to us both our sin and our reconciliation, both how far we are from God and how near God is to us in his love. The Cross is ever God's judgment upon the whole order of our life—as individuals, church, and society in general. When we let ourselves be judged and thereby broken loose from what we have been, *the Cross becomes the doorway to the new world* for which we long.

Paul emphasizes (vv. 9,10) that the Cross is

not only the means of our reconciliation with God but has as its fruit the reconciled and reconciling life that follows. We die with Christ to our old self-centered life that we may live with him to serve God and our fellow men! "Much more . . . shall we be saved by his life."

The two ages, or orders: the age of sin and death which began with Adam and the age of grace and life which began with Jesus Christ, are compared in Romans 5:12-21. Paul emphasizes and develops two points already established: the universality of sin in a human race that began with Adam and the intended universality of God's gift of grace, given through Jesus Christ to usher in a new age for all mankind. The similarity between Adam and Christ (that leads Paul in Romans 5:14 to call Adam a type of Christ) is that each stands at the head of a development in human life. But Paul's concern is more with the unlikeness of these developments: the one (from Adam) being a development of sin leading to death; the other (from Jesus) being an outpouring of the gift of grace issuing in life.

The reader must take care not to be misled by the opening sentence (5:12) of the section, for it breaks off when it has presented only the first

III

83

half of the comparison. Paul interrupts himself here, in verses 13 and 14, with a comment on the sway of sin in the world before the Law was given by Moses. The second half of the comparison begins in verse 15 and between verses 15 to 19 there are no fewer than five repetitions of the comparison. Paul says essentially the same thing over and over, to drive home his point, namely, that what has happened in Jesus Christ is nothing less than a fresh beginning for the entire human race. In the background of this comparison lies a rabbinic teaching concerning two Adams which appears more clearly in I Corinthians 15:45-49. The Adam of Genesis 2 and 3 is a living being, a man of dust (I Cor. 15:47) ; but the Adam of Genesis 1 bears the image of God and is "the man of heaven" (I Cor. 15:49) . Jesus, therefore, fulfills the promise of the "man of heaven" and stands in contrast to the "man of dust." As the last Adam, a life-giving spirit, he gives birth to a new race of men in his own likeness, which is the likeness of God.

The interjection in Romans 5:13-14, 20, contains a peculiar idea of Paul's concerning the law: that sin was in the world before the Law was given by Moses, but was not counted sin until the law identified it as such. The law, therefore, rather than overcoming sin, had the effect of increasing it. Sin, however, whether identified or not, had its deadly consequences. What Paul expresses is his personal disillusionment with the law as a legalistic way of obtaining salvation. From the vantage point of his own experience of grace, he looks back on what he now knows to be the futility and inability of the law to deal with the human problem of sin. The law, by generating a false confidence, blinded him and thereby increased the power of sin over him. Was it not the law which had provoked Paul in his blindness to become a persecutor of the Christians and provoked others to send Jesus to the cross? Paul may well be thinking of his own past when he writes, "where sin increased, grace abounded all the more" (5:20). No matter how great the power of sin may be, the power of grace is greater; the new Adam is certain of his triumph over the old.

FREEDOM FROM SIN

The Pauline doctrine of justification by faith has been misunderstood by some deluded persons in every generation, even Paul's own, as a permission to sin. Paul's negations concerning the law, which have to be understood in the light of his personal experience with a legalistic way of salvation, have perhaps encouraged this interpretation. Since faith alone counts with God, not one's obedience to the law, it might seem a matter of indifference whether one sin or not. If this were so, a statement such as, "where sin increased, grace abounded all the more," could be used as an argument that, by continuing to sin, one gave God renewed opportunities to exercise his grace. Paul, familiar with such perversion and twisting of his teaching meets it directly—in Romans 6.

Since he was dealing with Christians, all of whom had been baptized, his most effective argument was an exposition of the meaning of Christian baptism. The original form of baptism was probably taken over from Jewish proselyte baptism. The convert put off his clothes as a sign of putting off his old Gentile life and, going down into the water, was washed free of the old life to rise from the water, put on fresh clothing and enter upon his new life as a Jew. John the Baptist made of this rite a baptism of repentance for Jews, insisting thereby that they, too, needed to make as radical a change as any Gentile in order to participate in the coming new age of God. The adoption of baptism by the Christian movement as the ceremony of initiation made it for Jew and Gentile alike a sign of dying to one's former existence and coming to life in the new age of the Spirit. For John the Baptist baptism merely made one ready for the coming of the Spirit. For the Church baptism had as its essential meaning the receiving of the Holy Spirit (John 3:5; Acts 19:1-6), and was therefore a sign that one was entering the life of the new age.

Plainly, Paul's interpretation of baptism is not a distinctive doctrine of his own but a generally held Christian teaching. Christian faith is *faith in Christ crucified and risen*. But faith binds the believer to Jesus Christ so that Christ's death and resurrection are not events which occurred in the past—to which the believer merely looks back— but events in which he daily participates with his Lord. As Christ died to break the destructive reign of sin over man, the believer dies with him to sin and to his old sinful self; and as Christ rose from the dead to open to men a new age of grace, the believer rises with him into the new life of grace and of the Spirit. Therefore, if a baptized Christian considers his dependence upon grace and faith for his salvation as an encouragement to continue in sin, he shows an ignorance of the meaning of both grace and faith. Grace is mediated by a crucified and risen Lord; faith is the binding of the self to Christ, crucified and risen. Bound to such a Lord the believer is set free once and for all from the tyranny, but not from the temptation, of sin.

There was the danger, in emphasizing the Christian's freedom from the *reign* of sin (6:12), of seeming to suggest that by his conversion the Christian becomes free of all sin and is thus no longer a sinner. Paul's statement here has sometimes been interpreted in this way, in spite of his insistence elsewhere that temptation and sin remain a problem for the Christian to the very end of his journey.

Because the citizenship of the Christian is in the realm of grace and no longer in the realm of sin, Paul can say, "Consider yourselves dead to sin and alive to God in Christ Jesus" (6:11). But immediately thereafter (6:12), he appeals to those Christians (who by baptism have claimed this citizenship) not to let sin reign in them, not to obey their own passions. Paul is a realist, he has no illusions about what constitutes the life of a Christian. He knows there is no swift, easy passage into the full new age of grace. The Christian remains to his dying day a son of the first Adam, his life enmeshed in a world that is still under the tyranny of sin. His reconciliation with God does not set him free from his participation in the world, but rather deepens his sense of responsibility for its redemption. Because in Christ he has been freed from the *reign* of sin and brought under the reign of grace, a power is at work in and through the Christian to overcome sin and to make righteousness prevail in all human relations.

The accusation, therefore, that justification by faith encourages sin is an error and is senseless. The slave of Christ (the slave of righteousness), cannot at the same time be the slave of sin (6:17—18). The senselessness of any Christian letting himself become again enslaved by sin is nowhere more evident than in the fact that he would thereby surrender a life that is imperishable, a life beyond the reach of death. He would return to an existence which from beginning to end is under the curse of death (6:20-23).

WHAT PAUL ACHIEVED FOR HIS GENERATION HAS TO BE ACHIEVED
AFRESH EACH TIME THE FAITH IS ENDANGERED AS IT BLENDS
WITH THE CULTURAL ENVIRONMENT.   [95]

THE COMING OF CHRIST EXPOSES THE FULL DEPTH
OF THE DIVISION IN THE SELF. [100]

THE HUMAN SOUL IS A BATTLE-
GROUND ON WHICH THE WAR IS WAGED BETWEEN GOD AND ALL
THAT STANDS AGAINST GOD'S PURPOSE.   [100]

THE SPIRIT CAN BRING BOTH OUR CONSCIOUS
AND—WHAT IS OFTEN MORE IMPORTANT—
OUR UNCONSCIOUS NEEDS BEFORE GOD. [115]

THE LIBERATION OF MANKIND BRINGS WITH IT
THE LIBERATION OF THE WHOLE OF CREATION. [113]

THE SPIRIT FREES US NOT ONLY FROM OUR PAST
BUT ALSO FOR OUR FUTURE. [114]

SUFFERINGS THAT MIGHT HAVE
SEEMED PURELY DESTRUCTIVE CAN BE MADE TO SERVE ONE'S
PROGRESS TOWARD THE GOAL OF LIFE.   [115]

ETWEEN TWO WORLDS

   To understand Paul it is essential that we give his words the meaning which he gave them, not the meaning they currently are given. When Paul says, "The wages of sin is death," he is not saying, "If you sin you will one day die," a mild threat, since all men must one day die. Death here is the negation or absence of a life that is truly life. Sin robs life of its meaning, purpose, fulfillment. This is clear in Romans 7:11 where Paul says, "Sin . . . deceived me and killed . . . me." Again, 'death' and 'crucified' (6:3-6) describe the end, termination, of an old 'order of life.'

Another word which causes difficulty is 'flesh.' Sometimes Paul uses "in the flesh" to describe life in this world in contrast to life beyond the grave. But there are other times, as in Romans 7:5, when "in the flesh" stands in contrast to "in the Spirit" and refers to the old sinful order. (We must distinguish carefully between these two uses of the same word.) Paul also has his own way of using the term, 'law,' colored, as we have seen, by his experience of disillusionment with the legal code of Judaism as a way of salvation. Sometimes Paul uses 'law' to mean the whole complex law code, sometimes to mean Torah (strictly the first five books of the Old Testament, but sometimes used loosely in the New Testament for the whole of the Old Testament).

FREEDOM FROM LAW—FREEDOM AND LAW

The Christian life for Paul was characterized uniquely by its freedom. The Christian, by being bound to God in Christ, became the freest of all men. On the positive side Christians are free to fulfill their human destiny; on the negative side, they are free from the wrath of God, from sin, from the 'law,' and from 'death.' Romans 7 opens with Paul intent upon sharing his *freedom from the law* with the Roman Christians. He knows that they are familiar with the Jewish code of law (7:1), and he suspects that some have been attracted to a version of Christianity which tries to blend Christian faith with Jewish legalism.

We do not understand the problem which was faced here, nor do we recognize its modern parallels if we think of it only in terms of law and religious legalism. What was really happening was that some of the earliest Jewish Christians were attempting to hold their Christian faith within the framework of their traditional Jewish culture. A modern parallel, an example of the same thing, is seen in the attitude of American missionaries for whom the Christian faith becomes so blended with the American way of life that they consider themselves as much the representatives of a free enterprise system as of Christ. The British, in the past, were guilty of the same error, confusing the Empire's ideals and interests with Christian faith. Yet, it was perhaps the German blend of nationalism with Christianity in the German-Christian movement in the 1930's which most rudely awakened us to the seriousness of the problem.

Christians must necessarily live within some national culture, and the two traditions, the Christian and the national, inevitably become blended. The person who has grown up under the influence of both may be unable to distinguish one from the other. Both claim one's loyalty, but in the unconscious mixing and merging of the two, the values of the national culture may easily take precedence over the Christian elements so that a distinctively Christian faith becomes blurred or submerged.

Only by what is usually a painfully critical effort do Christians escape from this debilitating confusion. They do not have to deny or to become hostile to the culture and traditions of their nation, but they do have to let all of it come completely under the judgment of God's righteousness, that all of it may have the promise of God's salvation.

This problem of the relation between one's faith and one's national culture recurs, and must recur, in every age. Paul faced it in its earliest form. Law or Torah was the distinctive feature of Jewish culture. The fulfillment of life was sought by scrupulous obedience to the Torah. For Jews it provided the framework of daily life. They feared that its abandonment might reduce their world to chaos, just as today most Americans feel that the abandonment of the free enterprise system would mean the destruction of their world. Therefore some of the earliest Christians, as loyal members of the Jewish community, kept the framework of the Torah and built their new Christian existence within it. Had this practice prevailed the Christian faith would have been as inadequate to invade the non-Jewish world as a German- or British- or American-Christianity is to represent Christ in a non-Western world. Therefore, Paul's remarkable achievement in liberating the Christian faith from Jewish legalism was of crucial significance—not only for his mission to the Gentile world but for the whole subsequent history of the Christian church. And what Paul achieved for his generation has to be achieved afresh each time the faith is endangered by submergence and loss of character as it blends with its cultural environment.

We can understand Paul's eagerness, then, to liberate the Roman Christians from such a cultural servitude, especially since he hoped to make the Roman church his base for a mission to the Gentiles in the western region of the empire. The Jewish law, as a way of salvation, belonged to the old order of life which these Roman converts should have left behind when they were baptized as Christians. They had died to that world and were now free to live in a new order— just as a woman, bound by law to her husband, is free to marry again when death brings the former marriage to an end (vv.2-6). At the same time Paul had to guard against seeming to defame all law (vv.7-14). The law itself is God's law and is "holy and just and good" (v.11); but in a realm where sin reigns and determines the meaning of events, the law can be made to serve a purpose contrary to God's intention and become an instrument of death (v.11). The function of the 'Law' (a limited function in God's great order) was to give knowledge of sin, to make men aware of their sin (3:20; 7:7). It was never intended to be a way of salvation, and, when men sought salvation by obedience to it, instead of opening the way to God it blinded them to God and brought death upon them.

THE DIVIDED SELF

Many scholars have found it hard to believe that Paul was speaking out of his immediate Christian experience in Romans 7:14-25. They interpret the passage as a recollection of the inner struggle he endured in his pre-Christian days when he tried and failed to find salvation through obedience to the law. Though the verbs are all in the present tense, these scholars read them as though they were in the past tense: "I was carnal," "I did not understand my own actions," "Wretched man that I was." But this twisting of Paul's tenses presupposes that the Christian, who like Paul can say that he has passed from death to life, is no longer subject to the kind of dividedness, blindness, and confusion that Paul confesses here. By changing the tense, one misses the very point which Paul intends to make in this passage;

namely, that coming alive to God in Jesus Christ and entering upon the era of grace does not transport the Christian into 'nirvana' and end his confrontation with the power of sin in himself or in his world.

Moreover, to represent the pre-Christian Paul as engaged in a bitter internal struggle with himself is also contrary to the evidence. In Philippians 3:6 he recalls that he was a supremely confident Pharisee who considered himself blameless in his keeping of the law. As a Pharisee, Paul would have said, "The law is spiritual and I who who keep the law am spiritual, comparatively free from sin." But with the coming of Jesus Christ into his life, Paul's eyes were opened; he recognized his self-confidence as an illusion, a paralyzing illusion that robbed him of his destiny. He had been at peace with God too cheaply, like the Pharisee in Jesus' parable (Luke 18: 9-14) who "trusted in himself that he was righteous and despised others."

There are two seemingly contradictory sayings of Jesus concerning peace which need to be held together: "Come to me . . . and I will give you rest" and "I have not come to bring peace, but a sword." The parable just quoted shows how determined Jesus was to destroy the false and illusory peace of the religiously complacent. Jesus' crucifixion was due at least to some extent to the disturbance he caused in the minds of such people. They had made of their calling as a people of God a kind of safe religious harbor where they could ride at anchor and congratulate themselves upon standing so well with God. But they had lost from sight the purpose of God for mankind and for the world which they had been called to serve. They had lost all sense of how far they were from the fulfillment of the destiny which was the secret of Israel's distinctive and unique existence in the world. It was written plainly enough in the Torah and in the Prophets: Israel was set apart from other nations and preserved from extinction to be God's agent in bringing the light and blessing of the knowledge of God to all the nations (Gen. 12:1-3; Isaiah 42:6). Therefore an Israel pleased and content with its own superior righteousness had to be blasted loose from its complacency and set moving again toward its proper destination. That was the very revolution which confrontation with Jesus Christ had brought about in Paul, and each fresh confrontation made him aware of how far he had yet to travel in his journey from the old world to the new.

The parallel between the Israel of that day and the church of our day is so obvious that it need hardly be mentioned. All religion (including all forms of Christian religion) is in constant danger of becoming a complacent Pharisaism. Too often the moderately successful fulfillment of the moral and religious code makes Christians content with themselves and confident that God must be equally content with them. Any thought of being at God's disposal as the servant of his redemptive purpose, so that God may get on with his liberation of mankind from the forces that inhibit its humanity, is banished from the mind. The peace of a complacent Christian is like the peace of a stagnant pool which Christ must destroy if new life is to grow, if through them Christ is to make headway with his saving task.

For Paul to be "in Christ" was to stand before God and to know the full reality of the truth concerning himself; to know how far he still was from his destination—in spite of the grace he had received; to know how deeply his life was still webbed into the world of sin and death—in spite of his liberation from the tyranny of sin; and to realize how fragmented and incomplete was his knowledge of God—in spite of the light that had shone in upon him (I Cor. 13:12). It was the light that shone from the face of Jesus Christ that freed him from his illusions about himself and made him painfully conscious of how divided between the old world of sin and the new age of grace his existence still was.

There is no contradiction then between Paul's two assertions: "I am carnal, sold under sin" (7:14) and "the law of the spirit of life in Christ Jesus has set me free from the law of sin and death" (8:2). The apparent contradiction is a paradox which expresses the tension between the two worlds in which the Christian lives. Dissolve this tension and you put an end to the forward movement of the Christian from the old world to the new. Let us cease to know that we are "carnal, sold under sin," sinners enmeshed in a sinful world, desperately in need of redemption—and all too quickly we shall be anchored in complacency. Equally, let us lose sight of the new age for which Christ has set us free and there will no longer be any inner straining toward the goal (Phil. 3:12-14).

The coming of Christ does not put an end to the dividedness of the self but rather exposes the full depth of the division. We are torn between the forces of life and the forces of death. The human soul is a battleground on which the war is waged between God and all that stands against God's purpose in its justice, truth, and love. But Christ's coming transforms the dividedness *from a futile wavering* between life and death *into a decisive journey* out of death and into life. What sets us moving on that journey is the realistic recognition of the tenacity and deceptiveness with which sin and death continue their pressure on us throughout the entire course of our lives, to the very end.

Paul lets us see into his own inner struggle in Romans 7. In his mind and heart he is unconditionally committed to the will of God which is expressed in the law. Yet at times another will is at work in him, a will that produces deeds contrary to the will of God. Since these deeds are contrary also to what he himself wants to do, he has to disown the self that does them as an alien self empowered by sin (v. 20). In verses 21-23 he calls this alien power, the "law of sin." The will of God, in which his "inmost self" delights, he calls "the law of my mind." Two orders—one an order of death and the other an order of life— are in continuous conflict within him. Left to himself he would be in despair.

But Paul was not left to himself. His cry, "Who will deliver me from this body of death?" is like the cry of the publican in Jesus' parable, "God, be merciful to me a sinner!" When we remember Jesus' judgment that the publican who prayed, "God, be merciful to me a sinner!" went down to his house 'justified' (Luke 18:14), we realize how like-minded and close to each other were Jesus and Paul. In Romans 7:25 Paul gives thanks that in Jesus Christ he has assurance of his ultimate deliverance from sin and death and of his arrival at the destination of his journey—into life.

FREEDOM IN THE SPIRIT

Paul's mind leaps forward from the struggles of the journey which have been the burden of Romans 7 to the glory which awaits him at its destination (Rom. 8). He portrays in glowing colors the destiny of those who through faith in Christ are sharing the journey with him. We need to keep in mind that the new age is both present and future. The new age had this double character already in the preaching of a prophet such as Second Isaiah. He proclaimed the coming of a day when God's just and gracious rule would be established over all mankind, and at the same time he encouraged men to recognize that the rule was already hiddenly begun for them insofar as they remained open to God's word and Spirit (Isa. 45:22-24; 40:29-31). In like manner, the kingdom of heaven whose nearness Jesus announced, *was yet to come* in the future as the consummation and open triumph of God's purpose in the affairs of men and women. *But it was already present* as a new order or dimension of life in which the healing and transforming power of God's presence could be known *now*. The presence of the Kingdom was the presence of the King, God with man in Jesus Christ, a foretaste of the glorious future that God had in store for everyone. Thus, when Paul talks of the new age, he can move back and forth between present and future. For him the new age had its decisive beginning in the death and resurrection of Jesus and the outpouring of the Spirit, although he would not have denied its presence in the mission of Jesus. After all, Paul was prepared to see it foreshadowed in Abraham and in the faith of prophets and psalmists.

The new era is variously described as the 'Kingdom of God,' a 'new creation,' the 'righteousness of God,' 'the new age of the Spirit,' or simply as 'salvation'; but always it has a present and a future dimension. The present is broken and incomplete, but the future holds the resolution of all life's contradictions.

It is significant of Paul's way of thinking that he begins his description of life in the new age by declaring those who are "in Christ Jesus" to be free from God's wrath. Luther would have given freedom from wrath the same priority. But this expression, "freedom from wrath" will leave many present-day Christians unimpressed because they have never thought of themselves as being "under the wrath of God." They have been brought up to think of God's love as a beneficence which excludes any thought of wrath or judgment. Wrath and judgment seem to them to be concepts belonging to a primitive age, not to an enlightened age such as our own! Yet to separate God's love from his righteousness, his kindness from his severity, is to reduce it to a harmless sentimentality, no longer of any significance in understanding our experiences of life. God's wrath is the felt resistance of his will to the human will that sets itself against him. It is experienced as an impenetrable wall blocking our way into the future.

God's judgment is the exposure of our alienation from him in events which show our inability, by ourselves, apart from him, to make sense of our life or to realize a meaningful destiny. The wrath and judgment are almost tangible realities in our experience, both individual and collective, from time to time. They bring us into crisis. And if we banish these words from our vocabulary and our theology, we have no equipment with which to grapple with the realities they represent in present experience. Paul's 'good news' that we are free from the wrath of God becomes unintelligible. It has no point. In fact, Paul's entire gospel becomes pointless and innocuous when these realities are cancelled out. And not Paul's only. Jesus one day told men who were basking in God's favor that he could do nothing for them; he was sent only to those who knew their sickness and their sin (Mark 2:17), that is, who felt the burden of their alienation from God. Reconciliation meant forgiveness, the healing of the breach, the lifting of the burden.

The key words of Romans 8:1-17 are 'flesh' and 'Spirit.' It will help us to coordinate this passage with the preceding chapters if we recognize that Paul is still contrasting the old and new eras. Flesh denotes the total life of the old era, while "in the Spirit" indicates the total life of the new. Paul uses "in the Spirit" or "the Spirit in us" interchangeably to describe the new relationship with God upon which the Christian enters when he is bonded to Christ by faith. In the same way he uses "Christ in me" and "I in Christ" interchangeably to describe the same reality, for the Spirit can be called either "the Spirit of Christ" (8:9) or "the Spirit of God" (8:9, 14). This language has sometimes been understood to signify a mystic experience of absorption into God. But for Paul it always signifies a personal relationship in which the same Spirit of God that possessed Jesus and empowered him for his mission takes possession and mastery over the Christian and empowers him to carry forward the same mission. The 'Spirit' in the New Testament is never a vague, mystical, divine presence to be enjoyed by Christians only in their spiritual devotions. It is distinctively a presence of God with us that impels Christians who are so possessed to put themselves ever at the service of Christ for the extension of his mission.

The person who said that the Spirit for him was "a vague oblong blur" may speak for many Christians. God, the Father, makes sense to them. Jesus takes concrete form and commands their allegiance as they read of him in the Gospels. But the Spirit takes them beyond their depth and leaves them groping in a void. Yet the Spirit is the very power-center of the Christian gospel and the Christian faith. Vagueness at this point leaves us with an essentially powerless Christianity. That which made Jesus uniquely what he was, and empowered his being and mission, was the immediacy of God in him and the fullness of his life in oneness with the Father. His life on earth, from beginning to end, was "in the power of the Spirit" (Luke 4:14) . When he wished to share this life with others he could do so only by taking them with him into the mystery of his own life with God—a God no longer distant or vague but present and ready to transform human lives by the grace and power of his presence.

The Spirit is God in that form of his being in which he is no longer beyond us but comes to us and, within us, takes over the place of rule, thereby bringing us to the realization to our true selves and becoming a wellspring of imperishable life within us. The coming of the Spirit and the coming of God's kingdom are one and the same reality, for to receive the Spirit is to receive the King.

At the junction-point between the two worlds, the one of 'flesh,' and the other of 'Spirit,' stands Jesus Christ. Passage from one to the other is 'through' him. It is the "law of the Spirit of life in Christ Jesus" that sets us free from the law of sin and death (8:2). It is strange that Paul should speak of the 'law' of the Spirit but he does so most probably only in contrast to "the *law* of sin and death," pointing up the opposition of the two orders. What he is really thinking of is the *power* of God and the *action* of God in the person of Jesus, in his death and Resurrection, accomplishing what the law had been unable to do (v.3). To liberate mankind from a world of sin and death, Jesus, though he was one with God, the son of God, made himself one of us, and shared our human life to the full, taking upon himself the burden of our sinful world (v. 3. cf. Phil. 2:8). He became one with us that he might make us one with himself and with God, and the cost to him of his oneness with us was his cross.

In his death Jesus was God's judgment on the futility and alienation of the whole fleshly world and, at the same time, God's liberation from the tyranny of that world of all who let themselves come under the judgment. This meant liberation *from servitude to the law,* not into a life of *lawlessness* but into a life in the Spirit that richly fulfilled the requirements of God's law (8:4). The contrast of the two eras, verses 5-11, leads to an appeal to the Roman Christians (vv. 12-15) not "to live according to the flesh" nor "to fall back into fear" as though they had received "the spirit of slavery" instead of the Spirit of Christ.

To receive the Spirit is nothing less than to share with Christ his relation of sonship with the Father. This is the miracle of grace: that Christ takes us, sinners that we are, into the richness and joy and boundless hope of his own life in God. We are so bound together with him in the fulfillment of our destiny that we are heirs with him of the same glorious future. Then the warning comes (v. 17) that, if we are to share the glory with Christ in the future, we must be willing also to share the sufferings which are the cost of his redemptive mission in an alienated world.

To suffer with Christ is to serve with him. We have to see behind this reference to suffering not the ordinary suffering which is the human lot but the hatred, persecution, and special hardships which Christians, such as Paul, brought upon themselves by their unbending faithfulness in the Christian mission (II Cor. 11:23-29). To have evaded the suffering would have been to abandon the mission. There have been times in the life of the church when it seemed to enjoy such favor in the community that no one would ever have to suffer for his faith. Since the 1930's we have with good reason come to distrust such peace and placidity as purchased at the cost of compromise and concealment of the issues which Christ's new order raises for our established world. More recently in America when some of these issues have been forced into the open (and not always by Christians), faithfulness to Christ has again shown itself to be dangerous and costly.

The mention of present sufferings provokes Paul to a comparison of the embattled situation of the present with the glorious victory and consummation that await the sons of God in the future (8:18). It is true that we are now between two worlds, engrossed in a struggle, both in private and in public, between an order that is death-bound and a new order that has an infinite future. The struggle is sometimes bitter and discouraging. We become tempted to turn back and make our peace with the old order of flesh. But the whole perspective changes when we see the present struggle and suffering in the light of the goal toward which the Spirit of God is taking us. The new life which we have now as the gift of the Spirit is a foretaste of what is yet to come (v.23), and not just for ourselves as individuals but also for the Christian community. The book of Acts joins with Paul in emphasizing that life in the Spirit is not a spiritual experience which people are to enjoy alone in private, but is a new kind of life of person with person (Acts 2:44 ff.; 4:32).

People who are possessed and indwelt by the same Spirit of God have a common center for their existence in spite of all the things that might divide them. Their openness to God produces in them an openness to their fellow men. Because the Spirit has displaced the self from the place of rule at the center of their lives, they have a new self that is turned outward to the world. They are capable of a deeper sharing than had formerly been possible. In short, the Spirit at work within us creates a new kind of human community in which old divisions and prejudices are overcome, and we find ourselves, in spite of all distinctions, living together as children of one Father and servants of one Lord.

Paul had no illusions about the imperfections of this new order in even his best-loved churches (e.g., the Corinthian church) ; yet, what he saw of a new creation in them and in himself provided him with sure and sufficient promise of the ultimate transformation of the whole world—the final outcome of what was already begun.

Paul would have had no sympathy with a Christianity which confined its attention wholly to one's inner life and the saving of one's own soul, leaving life in the community—whether social, political or economic—to be ordered entirely by other authorities. He saw the whole creation, not just the world of men and women, but also the world of nature (ecology) , perverted from its true order by human blindness and sin, yet reaching out in longing for redemption and transformation. It is not just individual persons but a world that is waiting to be redeemed (Rom. 8:19) . This breadth of vision has a profound effect upon the character of the Church. Focused only upon the salvation of individuals, one by one, the Church tends to become a kind of island of refuge in the world, increasingly engrossed in its own life, turned inward upon itself. Knowing itself the instrument chosen by God for the rescue of mankind from self-destructive inclinations, and for the restoration of the world to its true destiny as God's good creation, the Church becomes turned outward to the world and is freed from unhealthy self-concern. The "eager longing" of the creation for its freedom from death and decay finds expression in a thousand ways if we have eyes to see and ears to hear—the cry of millions daily for bread enough to sustain life, the groaning of populations imprisoned under tyrannical forms of government, the protests of youth against established institutions which no longer meet their needs but refuse to change, the rebellion of racial minorities against the discrimination which impoverishes their life, the agony of soldiers and civilians debased and destroyed by senseless wars, the peril of air and water pollution caused by man's carelessness and greed. These are the sights and sounds of a creation "groaning in travail" for the coming of the new age. They *impel* the Church to take with full seriousness the dimensions of its calling.

"Groaning in travail," suggests birth-pains, a metaphor familiar elsewhere in Scripture. In

Isaiah 42:14 the prophet represents God himself as crying out in pain as he gives birth to a new age for Israel and for mankind. The Gospel of John describes the citizen of the new age as "born of God" or "born of the Spirit" (John 1:13 and 3:3). Paul sees both the individual Christian and the whole of creation as undergoing a process of rebirth as the age of sin and death is left behind and all move out into the freedom of the sons of God.

To Paul, rebirth is not a single experience, the moment of conversion, but the much more comprehensive and continuing movement out of death into life. The goal is "the revealing of the sons of God" (8:19) or "adoption as sons, the redemption of our bodies" (v.23) by which is meant the completion of the work of redemption, the creation of a race of men and women who will be as completely human as Christ was human, reflecting, as he did, the very nature of God.

The liberation of mankind brings with it the liberation of the whole of creation from futility. The interrelation of man's disorder with the disorder of nature has become much more vivid to us in recent years as ecologists have awakened us to our peril from the pollution and destruction of the natural environment. Paul stands in a biblical tradition which holds man responsible for his environment in the creation (Gen. 1:28; Ps. 8:6).

Upon what basis does Paul construct this vision of the future? Is it a dream, a speculation, a wish-construction? By no means. The first fruits of the new creation are already present in the Christian community (Rom. 8:23). What the Spirit has already achieved gives promise and confident hope of what is yet to come. The Christian lives in faith and hope and in the strength of his hope moves forward unafraid and undaunted by obstacles to claim his future destiny. The Spirit frees him not only *from* his past but also *for* his future.

There is a curious interjection in verses 26 and 27 (which seems to interrupt the flow of Paul's thought) concerning the helpfulness of the Spirit in one's intercessions with God. It is like a window into Paul's prayer life. At times, when he would approach God in prayer, he finds a weakness in himself in that he does not rightly understand how to pray. No words which he can frame are sufficient to express his need. But here, too, the Spirit brings freedom. The Spirit, being so completely "God with man," discerns the need before it can come to consciousness in words and becomes man's intercessor with the Father. We may be troubled that Paul seems to separate the

Spirit from God the Father, but it is only an indication of how deeply the Spirit interpenetrates the whole of our existence, and how in our prayers the Spirit can bring both our conscious and—what is often much more important—our unconscious needs before God.

THE VICTORY OF FAITH

The last two paragraphs of chapter 8 (vv. 28-30 and vv. 31-39) belong closely together, forming the climax of this section on life in the Spirit, the life of the new age. They must not be separated as though the first were a comment on predestination, and the second an exultant and defiant coda on the triumph of God's love in Christ over everything in heaven or earth that may stand against it. Nor should they be cut off from the whole development of thought which has preceded. Here the good news which Paul has been unfolding from the first words of his letter reaches its highest pitch.

The new age of the Spirit is the vindication of God's righteousness, for in it we, responding in love to the love of God, find that God makes everything work together for good. Sufferings that might have seemed purely destructive are made to serve one's progress toward the goal of life (5:3-5). A cross that outwardly seemed to be a tragic defeat becomes the primary instrument of God's conquering power (I Cor. 1:18, 24). The rejection of the gospel by Paul's fellow Jews hastens its acceptance by the Gentiles (Rom. 11:11, 25).

In "everything" Paul includes all of life's experiences without exception. For those adrift in an alien world, these are divided into fortunate experiences and experiences that can be endured only as the buffetings of a cruel fate. Both kinds of experience leave us where we are. But to those who are indwelt by the Spirit, caught up by it into the movement of humanity out of slavery into freedom, every experience, positive and negative alike, is made to serve the unfolding of God's purpose and to carry them toward their goal.

Verses 29 and 30 of chapter 8 trace out the comprehensive arc of the Christian's journey. Before ever he hears the call of God, God's care for him has overshadowed his life. In Galatians 1:15 Paul, like Jeremiah (Jer. 1:5), speaks of being set apart by God for a particular service before he was born. Here (Rom. 8:29) he applies the same conception to every Christian. Each has his particular destiny to fulfill within the total purpose of God for the redemption of mankind. The words "foreknew" and "predestined" are not to be interpreted in fatalistic terms as though the events of time were merely the unfolding of a minutely predetermined plan, or as though the purpose of God included in its scope only a favored few of the human race. God's purpose, as we have already seen, is for the whole creation. And the way his purpose unfolds is dependent, in a high degree, upon the response of men and women in faith. It is the destiny of all "to be conformed to the image of his Son, in order that he might be the first-born among many brethren."

In verse 30 Paul marks out again the stages in the journey from the old world and the old self to the new world and the new self. The first stage, covering the long ages of preparation for man's redemption, reaches back to the creation and forward to the beginning of the new creation in Jesus Christ. Then God's call to man in the preaching of the gospel and the justification or reconciliation of those who respond to God's call in faith, forms the second stage. But this is only the beginning of the journey. What God has begun by reconciling men to himself in Christ, he eventually completes when sin is finally overcome and men share fully in the divine glory in Christ.

Christians embarked on such a glorious destiny

have their enemies and their detractors who try to dissuade them from their course, sometimes by persecution. How can they give way, however, when the power of God, sovereign in creation, is on their side and makes all things, even the death of his own Son, serve his gracious purpose for them? Why should they heed men's scorn and condemnation when already they stand fully justified before God? Their faith unites them with Christ and makes Christ their intercessor with God. No misfortune that may befall them can separate them from the love of Christ. In the security of that love, they can make their journey toward their goal like conquerors. Nothing in heaven or earth, not even death, can separate them from that love in Christ which is the love of God for all his creation.

IN AN ASCRIPTION OF PRAISE (ROMANS 11:33-36), PAUL MAR-
VELS AT THE MYSTERIOUS WAYS IN WHICH GOD UNFOLDS HIS PUR-
POSE FOR MANKIND—MAKING ALL THINGS ULTIMATELY SERVE
HIS WILL.   [143]

FAITH IS FAITH IN THE LIVING GOD
WHO IS WORKING OUT HIS PURPOSE FOR MAN
IN THE WHOLE OF HISTORY.   [129]

FAITH, ACCORDING TO JESUS,
SO LINKS GOD WITH MAN THAT IT
CAN MOVE MOUNTAINS. [152]

ROMANS 10:14-21 IS PAUL'S ARGU-
MENT FOR THE GENTILE MISSION. IF GOD HAS SPOKEN THE WORD
IN CHRIST THAT OFFERS SALVATION TO EVERYONE WHO RESPONDS
TO IT IN FAITH, THEN THE WORD MUST BE PREACHED IN ALL
THE WORLD.   [140]

THE COMING OF CHRIST MARKS THE
GREAT TURNING POINT IN GOD'S
WORK OF UNIVERSAL SALVATION. [139]

IT WAS WITHIN THE REMNANT
(GOD'S FAITHFUL FEW) THAT THE
FAITH WAS KEPT ALIVE. [123]

IF WE ARE TO SHARE THE GLORY WITH
CHRIST IN THE FUTURE, WE MUST BE WILLING ALSO TO SHARE
THE SUFFERINGS, THE COST OF HIS REDEMPTIVE MISSION IN AN
ALIENATED WORLD.   [108]

chapter V

CHRISTIAN AND JEW

Paul wrote his letter to Rome more than 20 years after the death of Jesus. By that time it was clear that the mass of the Jewish people had rejected the Christian gospel. Both in Palestine and in the lands of the dispersion only a handful of Jews were found in the Christian Church. Already the Church had become preponderantly a Gentile church. This was both a sorrow and a mystery to Paul. It was a sorrow because to him the faith generated in men by Jesus Christ was the climax and fulfillment of the faith that had been at the core of Israel's life from the beginning. It was "promised [by God] beforehand [through his prophets] in the holy scriptures" (Rom. 1:2). "The law and the prophets bear witness to it" (3:21). Abraham and David were models of it long centuries before its flowering in the gospel (Rom. 4).

What made Paul a Christian was not just a miraculous vision of the risen Lord but a recognition that what had happened in the ministry, death, and resurrection of Jesus and what was happening among his disciples was the continuation of the redemptive action of God that in the past had given Israel its special mission as the chosen people. He awakened to the realization that Israel, lulled into complacency by pride in its heritage, had lost sight of its destiny as the agent of God's purpose on behalf of all mankind. Jesus as the Christ, breaking open the way into the future, was recalling Israel to its historic destiny. Therefore, in becoming a Christian Paul did not become any less a Jew, nor did he cherish any the less his Jewish Scriptures and traditions. For the converted Paul the Christian was the Jew *par excellence,* with a true understanding of the Jewish scriptures which had long been obscured in traditional interpretations (II Cor. 3:14). Paul sorrowed, therefore, that so many of his fellow Jews remained unawakened to what was most certainly their promised future. They were unaware of the new era in the life of man that had dawned in their very midst.

This tragic blindness of his fellow Jews, which separated them from him and made them treat him as a dangerous enemy, continued to puzzle and trouble Paul. It was not only a sorrow to him, it was also a mystery. In the thousand years and more of Israel's history, in every generation there had been blindness, unfaithfulness, and frequently rejection of those who undertook to speak for God to the nation. It was almost a tradition that Israel at first rejected any new prophet who, in the name of God, opposed the established order and pointed the way into the future. Later, however, after such prophets were dead, they were honored and their messages preserved for future generations. Moreover, there had never been a time when more than a remnant of the nation had a true understanding of Israel's vocation as the people of God. It was within this remnant that the faith was kept alive. The official rejection of Jesus, then, had been in line with the traditional response of Israel to servants of the Word; but the usual posthumous reversal of the nation's judgment and the recognition of his validity as God's spokesman had been only fragmentary. Why had not *all* experienced the same reversal of judgment as Paul did? How could any Jew fail to see that Jesus brought the whole Old Testament development to its consummation and set it moving toward a new goal? How could anyone be blind to the fact that, in carrying forward the mission of Jesus, the church was performing the task which the prophets had assigned to Israel, letting the light of the knowledge of God shine out to the ends of the earth?

The stubbornly continuing blindness of his fellow Jews was, therefore, a mystery to Paul; he found it almost impossible to understand. His belief in the sovereignty of God made him ask whether, in some strange way, this blindness of Israel might be serving God's larger purpose. He was familiar with the account in Exodus of how God blinded Pharoah to what would have been for his own good in order to open the way for Israel to escape from Egypt. Was, then, Israel's present blindness only temporary in order to divert the gospel from the narrow Jewish enclave to the wider Gentile world? Was God's intention, not that the Jews should be left behind, but that they would be built in later into the broadened movement of their own historic faith. In Romans 9-11 Paul expresses his conviction that it is unthinkable that Jew and Christian should long remain alienated from each other. So passionate is his love for his own people that, though nothing is more precious to him than the life he has in Christ, he would be willing to be accursed and cut off from Christ (9:3) if thereby the eyes and hearts of his people might be opened to the gospel. What, then, must be God's intention for this people which has been the object of his love throughout the centuries, a people with which he has had to be so patient and forgiving? He has not borne with them for a thousand years to cast them aside now. No! They, too, must share in the glorious future that God has prepared. The movement of his grace has passed them by only for the moment in order to reap a harvest among the Gentiles. Surely, very soon, the hour will come when they will be gathered in to enrich the life of the larger Israel of the future.

PAUL'S HOPE DELAYED

More than nineteen centuries have passed since Paul expressed confidence in a comprehensive reconciliation of Christian and Jew. Yet hostility between them has more often been the order of the day. At first in the Roman Empire it was a hostility on the part of the more numerous Jewish population toward the struggling little Christian churches, but as the Christian community became larger and more powerful, the order was reversed and Jews began to suffer penalties for their Jewishness. These they have continued to endure within the so-called Christian world throughout all succeeding centuries.

At various times, in various places, there have been islands of peace where Jews and Christians have lived together with mutual respect and a considerable degree of co-operation, but these have been no more than islands within seas of hostility which the Jew has felt might at any moment sweep in upon him to annihilate him. The murder of millions of Jews in Europe less than forty years ago—while Christians looked on and did little or nothing to provide places of refuge—still contributes to an atmosphere of fear. There are organizations today on this continent that steadily grind out a literature of vicious hatred and defamation directed at the Jew. Some of them even dare to call themselves Christians!

What is perhaps still more serious is the unreasoning and often unconscious antipathy to Jews (unless they happen to be entertainers or musicians) present in so many Christians that is like an inherited poison in their bloodstream. If this antipathy does not issue in any overt hostility, at the least it makes them indifferent to the problem of the relation between Christians and Jews.

When Christians do become concerned about their Jewish brethren, that concern is only too likely to take the form of an attempt to convert them from Judaism to Christianity, an endeavor which has been notoriously unsuccessful through the years and which, while it may bring a few Jews into the Church, has had the effect of further alienating the Jewish population as a whole. Quite understandably! A Christian church that has not yet dealt forcefully with the problem of its own members' hostility to Jews is hardly credible as a messenger of the love of God for all mankind revealed in Jesus Christ. From the standpoint of the Jew, a Christian mission for his conversion is not an expression of love and understanding, but rather is evidence of a religious imperialism which insults his faith and is interested only in removing the annoyance of a Jewish constituency in our society.

A more humane and a less self-righteous expression of concern is the opening up of conversations between Christians and Jews that the two may better understand each other, removing wherever possible occasions of conflict or distrust, exploring points of mutually desirable cooperation in the life of the modern community, and in general keeping open the channels of communication. But it is shocking that such conversations should only have begun in recent years and disappointing that they should sometimes prove so difficult to maintain. In many communities there is no attempt from either side to converse. The church and the synagogue go their separate ways in complete indifference to each other. This has had tragic consequences in the past and could have them again in the future, tragic not only for the Jew who is destroyed but for the Christian who by his silence and indifference cooperates with the destroyer. A Christian who shares the faith of Paul, and who has even the slightest consciousness of what it means that his faith comes to him from a nation of Jews, cannot be content to leave that gulf between Christian and Jew. The initiative must be his, but he will need to undergo a searching self-examination before he acts if he is not to widen the gulf in his attempt to bridge it. It may be that Paul in Romans 9-11 can help prepare us for the encounter.

PAUL'S HISTORICAL PERSPECTIVE

The break between Romans 8 and Romans 9 is so sharp some commentators have regarded Romans 9 through 11 as a separate document inserted between the preceding and following chapters. Chapter 8 brings the argument of the book to a triumphant conclusion—the faith that God has opened to man in Jesus Christ carries life to its unconquerable fulfillment in time and in eternity. But Paul has already made it plain that the community of faith has its roots in Israel's past. The new era now dawning had been foreshadowed in Abraham, David, the prophets, and the psalmists as representatives of a faithful Israel—foreshadowed in such a way that men could already experience something of the life of the time that was yet to come. God's action for man's salvation did not begin with Jesus. It reached its climax in his death and resurrection. But that climax (in Jesus) was recognizable only in continuity with the saving action of God in the life of Israel across the centuries.

Salvation had a history and it was to have a further history, for the consummation of the new era, the redemption of the whole creation—the final goal of God's action—still lay in the future. The agent of God's action in history, the community in which faith was nurtured and through which it was propagated, had for centuries been Israel. Now, however, the word and action of God in the gospel generated by Jesus had burst out beyond the confines of Israel, with all mankind as its goal. A new community of faith was coming into existence as the agent of God's action in history. *Faith* is faith in the living God who is working out his purpose for man in the whole of history. That purpose is manifest supremely in Jesus Christ; and to have faith in Christ is to put oneself at God's disposal in the service of his purpose, to have one's life used in the unfolding of what is no less than the redemption of the whole creation.

Salvation, then, is a movement, a development, a growth, in history. It is something happening in time that is so vast that it can have its full consummation only beyond time. In Romans 11:17ff. Paul gives expression to this historical perspective in the image of the olive tree. Israel as the people of God, called to serve him in history, is like an olive tree with its roots deep in the soil. Gentiles who become Christians are like branches broken off from a wild olive tree and grafted into the cultivated olive tree of Israel. The church is a true church only insofar as it preserves this continuity with the past. It is not a new and different Israel; it is simply the genuine Israel with no justification for its distinctive existence except that it is open and responsive to the continuing word and action of God in history. An Israel that cannot hear God's word in the gospel or recognize his action in the conversion of the Gentiles is an Israel that, for the moment at least, has lost sight of its destiny and is missing its calling. There have always been Israelites who have missed their calling, who have been like branches broken from the olive tree. But the olive tree of a historically rooted Israel remains, has ever remained and must ever remain, indestructible, rooted not in man's intention but in God's action, calling into being in every generation a people for his service. If Christians by their blindness and unresponsiveness cease to serve, they in turn will become branches broken from the olive tree, needing like the Jewish branches to be grafted in again.

Perhaps now we can see how naturally for Paul the discussion of the destiny of Israel, in Romans 9 through 11, follows on the exposition of justification by faith alone in Romans 1 through 8. We have noted how sensitive he was to the charge that, in becoming a Christian and an apostle to the Gentiles, he had betrayed his own historic heritage. In answer to this charge he insists that the circumcision of the heart which Christ effects is the only true circumcision (Rom. 2) , that it is a faith like Abraham's that makes one a son of Abraham (Rom. 4) , and that the continuity of the true Israel of God is maintained not by any legal devices but only by an openness to the leading of the Spirit. He has not turned his back on his heritage or on the sacred

Scriptures of Israel but, in his preaching of a grace that reaches out to take in all mankind, he is most faithful to the intention of those Scriptures and to the purpose for which God originally called Israel into existence. The gospel he proclaims is so profoundly at one with the witness to God of patriarchs, prophets, and psalmists in the past that it is unthinkable that any who call themselves Israelites should long remain impervious to its appeal.

If we sketch the history of salvation as it existed in Paul's mind, then, we would find ourselves with a predominantly Jewish history. For more than 1500 years, from Abraham to Christ, it is exclusively Jewish, with the Christ himself a Jew. The mission to the Gentiles widens the scope to take in all mankind, but Paul expected that mission soon to provoke the envy of his fellow countrymen (11:14) and to bring about the conversion of at least some of them. His firm conviction was that, when the harvest among the Gentiles was gathered, the Jewish people would embrace the gospel, participating with the Gentiles in the consummation of the history. He did not expect the Gentile interim to be long, perhaps not as long as his own lifetime. Paul's concept of the history of salvation, therefore, would look something like this diagram.

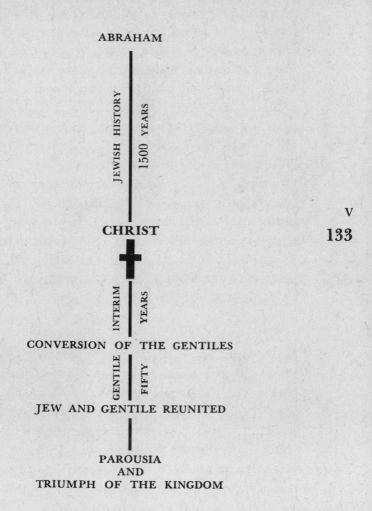

ABRAHAM

JEWISH HISTORY 1500 YEARS

CHRIST

INTERIM YEARS

CONVERSION OF THE GENTILES

GENTILE FIFTY

JEW AND GENTILE REUNITED

PAROUSIA
AND
TRIUMPH OF THE KINGDOM

V

133

A church which thinks of its history as almost exclusively Gentile, with only a vague Israelite prelude, and with a Christ whose Jewish race has to be called to mind with an effort, a church which no longer considers the Jew as well as the Christian to have an essential place in the history of salvation, has abandoned the Pauline view of things. Two communities which in the divine plan belong most intimately together have been allowed to diverge widely. The Jew who excluded the Gentile has been replaced by the Gentile Christian who *excludes* (or at least *forgets*) the Jew, and who, in many instances today, forgets the centuries of Jewish history in which his own existence as a Christian is rooted. The too frequent abandonment of the Old Testament in the Church is just one aspect of the abandonment of the Jew.

THE SOVEREIGN FREEDOM OF GOD

In the opening paragraph of chapter 9 (9:1-5), Paul calls to mind the uniqueness of Israel's relation with God. Israel is bound to him by covenants and promises (some texts have "the covenant" and "the promise"), entrusted with the Torah, called "my son" (Ex. 4:23) by God. It knows the glory of God's presence and the joy of pure worship. He then hastens to deal with the problems raised by Israel's failure to respond to God's word in Christ. Has the word of God failed (v. 6)? Has God been unjust in passing by his chosen people (v. 14)? Paul's answer is that God has always preserved his freedom of action even in relation to Israel. Israel has been bound to God; but God has not bound himself to every Israelite, the faithful and the unfaithful alike. Never in the past have all Israelites belonged to the true and faithful Israel. Isaac belonged, but not Ishmael; Jacob, but not Esau.

This selectiveness on God's part provokes the questioning of his justice. Is it fair that he should choose the one and reject the other? To this Paul answers that God's choice is determined by his mercy and compassion and he illustrates his point with the story of the Exodus. God's great act of mercy in liberating his people from Egypt had as its counterpart the hardening of the heart of Pharaoh; mercy for the one and judgment for the other. So now, his great mercy toward the Gentiles, liberating them through the gospel from the world of sin and death, has had as its counterpart the hardening of Jewish hearts against the gospel. "He has mercy upon whomever he wills" (vs. 18).

The emphasis upon the sovereignty of God in the events of history, here and elsewhere in scripture, has sometimes led to a deterministic doctrine of predestination, as though the attitudes and actions of men were pre-determined directly by God, as though God arbitrarily chose one man for salvation and another for damnation. On the contrary, the basic biblical understanding of the personal relationship between God and man is that man is called to respond to God in freedom, and that in the realm of history men *can* say "No!" to God, which excludes any deterministic conception. There are no puppets in the biblical story. Things do not happen by divine prearrangement. And yet God remains sovereign in the events, using even the anger of those who resist him to set forward his saving purpose.

The stubborn blindness of Pharaoh is made to issue in the liberation of Israel from Egypt. The stubborn blindness of Israel in relation to Jesus is made to issue in the liberation of the whole world from darkness and death. The divine control is not to be conceived as a manipulation of puppets but rather as the power to determine the ultimate issue of every event. A Pilate, a Judas, and a Jerusalem council can nail the Savior of the world to a cross but it is God who decides what that cross is to mean in the subsequent history of mankind.

In verse 19 Paul recognizes that what he has written seems to make God responsible for the Jewish rejection of the gospel and that, on that basis, criticism of the Jews for their rejection would hardly be fair. To meet this objection, he resorts to the prophetic likening of Israel's relation to God to that of a pot to its maker (Isa. 29:16; 45:9). The image is unsatisfactory; it makes God's relation to man like the control of an inanimate thing and therefore encourages a deterministic conception of God's sovereignty in history. The simple fact is that Paul is puzzled by the mystery of the failure of the Jews to see God's saving action in Jesus and his gospel. Though he can see what God has made of that failure, he has to leave the failure itself hidden in the mystery of the divine freedom. God does what he will with what is his own creation.

Quickly, however, Paul gets back to the theme of God's mercy (Rom. 9:23). All that God does has as its goal the extension of his mercy until it enfolds all mankind. A quotation from Hosea is reinterpreted. "Those who were not my people," is understood no longer merely as alienated Israel but as the whole Gentile world, to whom the promise is now given that they shall be "my people" and "my beloved."

Finally, in 9:30-33, he removes all arbitrariness from God's action: the Gentiles have moved into a place of precedence because of their openness in faith to God's righteousness and the Jews have been displaced because of their blindness to God's righteousness, intent upon establishing their own righteousness on the basis of law. The gospel of salvation by grace through faith has been a stumbling block in their path which has occasioned their failure. God's mercy must have its freedom to find its way past all obstacles to its destination.

Thus while Romans 9 first seemed to introduce a new subject, its closing verses show it to be only the development of a new phase of the original theme "God's righteousness through faith." The true Israel of God in every generation is a community that is unconditionally at the disposal of God as he invades the world with his transforming righteousness, not a community turned in upon itself in its concern with its own religiousness.

We are unfair if we apply this principle only to the situation of Paul's day. What Paul says of his contemporary Jews he could say of many present-day Christians, that "they have a zeal for God but it is not enlightened" (10:2). They are "ignorant of the righteousness that comes from God" and in their ignorance are intent upon establishing their own righteousness in the sight of both God and man (10:3). They are not interested in putting themselves at God's disposal for the invasion of the world with his new order.

It is not easy to follow Paul's line of thought in Romans 10. He begins, as he did in chapter 9, by expressing his passionate longing that his fellow Jews may all share in the new age, and by acknowledging the earnestness of their devotion to God. But with all their devotion they remain blind to the fact that a new day is dawning, that in Christ the era of Jewish righteousness in obedience to Jewish law has come to an end. They will not recognize that God has opened the way for all men to share freely in his gift of a righteousness which is life in the strength and richness of his own Spirit. The life and death of Christ marks the great turning point in God's work of universal salvation. The key to the chapter lies in verse 4. In Christ the action of God for the world's redemption has burst through the boundaries of Judaism and is moving out to the ends of the earth to make faith possible for "every one." Christ is "the end of the law" in the sense that he has made the legalistic religion of the former era obsolete.

In 10:5-13 Paul calls up two passages from the

Pentateuch to support his argument. The first, from Leviticus 18:5, shows that the intention of the law was that, by obedience to it, men might live and not die. The second, from Deuteronomy 30:12-14, in its original form assured men that the word of God which is the source of life does not have to be sought in the heavens or beyond the seas but is close to their hearts. Paul reinterprets this passage to emphasize and to witness to the nearness of the risen Lord from whom comes the true righteousness and life. Thus, with one quotation after another from the Old Testament, the sacred Scriptures of Judaism (two other quotations follow in verses 11 and 13), Paul insists that the Torah itself (the Law, the Pentateuch) points forward to the new era in which salvation is to be offered freely to all men.

Romans 10:14-21 is, therefore, Paul's argument for the Gentile mission. If God has spoken the word in Christ that offers salvation to everyone who responds to it in faith, then that word must be preached in all the world. Using a quotation from Joel 2:32 as an anchor point (9:13), Paul ingeniously constructs a chain of interlocking questions in verses 14-15, to show the impossibility of God's work of salvation coming to universal fruitage unless there is a community that knows itself commissioned to preach the gospel to every man. "Faith comes by hearing," (NEB) though not all who hear respond (v. 16). But already the gospel has been preached far and near (v. 18) and Gentiles have responded in such a way that it should make Israel jealous (vv. 19, 20). A final quotation in verse 21 expresses Paul's sorrow that Israel now, as in the past, resists the appeal of God.

Paul introduces no new argument in Romans 11 but drives home with hammer blows the points he has already made. He denies absolutely that God has rejected Israel as his chosen people. Their blindness to the truth is a temporary blindness. "The gifts and the call of God are irrevocable" (v. 29). Even now, in spite of their hostility to the gospel, the Jewish people are still God's "elect," "beloved for the sake of their forefathers" (v. 28). If their rejection of the gospel has served God's greater purpose by diverting the Christian mission to the Gentile world, their ultimate acceptance of it and reunion with the Christian church will be an even more glorious triumph for God (v. 15). Not for one moment will Paul consider the possibility that the old Israel, though at present a stubbornly resistant Jewish people, has come to the end of its history as God's servant people to be replaced by the Christian Church. There have been earlier times when the nation as a whole seemed to reject its destiny and so to have lost its future. But always God preserved for himself a faithful remnant in which the knowledge and love of his truth were kept alive. Elijah in his despondency had thought that he alone remained faithful in a degenerate age but, hidden from him and known only to God, there were seven thousand who were still unswervingly loyal to their God (Rom. 11:2-4). Likewise, Paul insists, there is now a remnant, "chosen by grace," responsive to God's call, standing in continuity with the servant Israel of the past but hidden now within the largely Gentile church. And with this remnant, Paul foresees, the whole of Israel will one day be reunited.

One gets the impression that in the whole section, verses 13-32, Paul is combatting a tendency of Gentile Christians to disparage their continuity with Israel and to regard the Jewish people as abandoned by God because of their attitude to the gospel. One aspect of his mission to the Gentiles, Paul says, is that by their conversion he may make his fellow Jews jealous and win them to Christianity. Those who have already become Christian are like the portion of dough "offered to God as first fruits," which will eventually make all of the dough, i.e., the whole of Israel, holy (v. 16). Changing the metaphor, he speaks of this Jewish remnant as the root and trunk of Israel, of which all Jews are branches. Branches may have been broken off because of their rejection of Christ but they still belong to the root and share the holiness of the root. Moreover, these Jewish branches still belong by nature to the tree of Israel and, though broken off, they can more readily be grafted back into the tree than can the Gentile branches (v. 24). Over and over Paul insists that Gentile Christians must never forget that the diversion of the Christian mission from the Jews to the Gentiles, to bring about *their* reconciliation with God, was a direct consequence of the Jewish alienation (vv. 1,15, 19,30). Therefore, Gentiles must join with Paul in eager longing and prayer for a reconciliation of Jews and Christians. Paul closes the discussion with an ascription of praise (11:33-36) in which he marvels at the mysterious ways in which God unfolds his purpose for mankind, making all things ultimately serve his will.

CHRISTIAN AND JEW TODAY

We can suggest only briefly the implications of Paul's thought for our relation with the Jewish people of today.

First, we must recognize the extent to which

the church has become what Paul deplored: a Gentile church that is indifferent to its foundations in the Israel of the Old Testament and inclined to regard Judaism as just one among the many non-Christian religions of mankind. Christians will never have a right attitude toward Jews as long as they are allowed to remain ignorant of the rootage of their Christ, and of every aspect of their faith, in the Israel of the Old Testament. A thorough understanding of this Israel can generate sound respect for a people that still draws its inspiration and guidance from the Old Testament and can make clear how much Christians and Jews have in common. He who truly responds in faith to the words of Moses or Amos or Jeremiah already responds, whether he knows it or not, to the word which we hear in Jesus Christ (cf. John 5:46).

Second, if we agree with Paul that God has not abandoned the Jews, that their blindness is temporary, and that we are to share with them in the consummation of God's redemptive purpose for mankind, we shall no longer maintain the customary Christian attitude of indifference or exclusion toward Jewish people. We are bound to each other by our separate binding to the God of the Scriptures. If we, Christians and Jews alike, know ourselves to be the servant people of God in continuity with the Israel of the Scriptures, then we cannot be more than temporarily apart from each other. Just as within the Church there are divisions that are yet to be overcome, so in the more comprehensive Israel of God there are divisions yet to be healed. Faith already sees a unity in spite of division and embraces it in hope of a richer future.

We shall begin to ask ourselves, then, what it has been in the witness of the Christian church that has prolonged the alienation of the Jews far beyond anything anticipated by Paul? At the time of the exodus they rebelled against Moses; and then they recognized him as their God-given leader. Elijah had to flee for his life; but, after his death, he became the great prophet-hero of his people. Jeremiah so offended the people of Jerusalem that they called him a traitor and tried to kill him; but as time went on, his sermons became a part of their sacred scriptures. Paul had good reason to expect that before long his nation as a whole would recognize in Jesus the fulfillment of the profoundest hopes of their history and the richest promise for their future. Why has his expectation remained unfulfilled? Why does it still seem far from fulfillment? The answer is not far to seek. A Christian church and a supposedly Christian society which have consistently through the centuries exposed the Jews to varying degrees of discrimination and persecution, and still nourish a smouldering element of distrust and hostility, have concealed, and still conceal from the Jew, the face of Jesus Christ!

V
146

CHRISTIAN LOVE IS THE FULFILL-
MENT OF THE LAW. [157]

TO BE IN CHRIST, IS TO HAVE THE
"MIND" OF CHRIST, TO SEE ALL THINGS FROM A NEW VANTAGE
POINT, TO DO ONE'S THINKING FROM A NEW CENTER. THEN, IN-
STEAD OF CONFORMING EASILY, ONE IS READY TO PROBE INTO AN
AS-YET-UNDISCOVERED FUTURE TO FIND WHAT GOD'S WILL HAS
IN STORE. [153]

THE MARK OF THE CHRISTIAN IS HIS FREEDOM
FROM ALL SELF-RIGHTEOUSNESS. [167]

HOW CAN WE RECEIVE THE FORGIVING
AND RECONCILING LOVE OF GOD OURSELVES UNLESS WE ARE
WILLING TO MEET OUR NEIGHBORS WITH THE SAME FORGIVING
AND RECONCILING LOVE? [159]

A FAILURE TO USE ONE'S GIFTS
IS AS REPREHENSIBLE AS AN
OVER-ESTIMATION OF ONE'S GIFTS. [156]

WE CAN BE SURE THAT FAITH HAS EQUIPPED
EVERY CHRISTIAN WITH SOME CAPACITY FOR
THE SERVICE OF CHRIST. [156]

PAUL WAS AWARE THAT THE CONSTANTLY DISRUPTIVE FACTOR IN LIFE'S RELATIONSHIPS WAS HUMAN EGOTISM: SELF-CENTERED-NESS, PRIDE, THE DRIVE OF THE SELF TO BE ITS OWN MASTER. [154]

WE CAN ONLY FORM A RIGHT ESTIMATE OF OURSELVES WHEN WE SEE OURSELVES AND OUR RELATIONSHIPS AS THEY APPEAR TO US WHEN WE ARE IN GOD'S PRESENCE. [156]

THROUGH THE CENTURIES MEN FOUND IT EASIER TO OFFER SOMETHING OTHER THAN THEM-SELVES TO GOD—AN ANIMAL SACRIFICE (OR EVEN A HUMAN SACRIFICE), A BEAUTIFUL RITUAL, A TITHE OF THEIR INCOME, A PARTIAL OBEDIENCE——

BUT THE PROPHETS INSISTED THAT THE ONE TRUE SACRIFICE WAS THE HUMBLE AND CONTRITE HEART, OPEN UNCONDITIONALLY TO GOD'S WILL AND PROVING ITS INTEGRITY BY A STEP BY STEP OBEDIENCE. [152]

HUMAN PRIDE CAN, IN A MOMENT, CHANGE RIGHTEOUSNESS INTO SELF-RIGHTEOUSNESS AND DISRUPT THE FELLOWSHIP THAT FAITH HAS BROUGHT INTO BEING. [167]

IN A COMMUNITY WHERE LOVE PREVAILS, THE STRONG WILL ACCEPT LIMITATIONS ON THEIR FREEDOM IN ORDER TO PROTECT THE WEAK. [169]

chapter VI

CHRISTIAN BEHAVIOR IN THE NEW AGE

Just as a new theme seemed to begin in Romans 9, so also in Romans 12 we seem to be launched on a new subject. Chapters 12 through 15 of Romans address themselves very concretely to the question of how Christians in the new age are to relate to each other and to the world in which they live—in short, the ethical question. But both sections (Rom. 9-11 and 12-15) are developments of the main theme: the righteousness of God which, through Christ, creates a new humanity and a new human community. In Romans 9 through 11 the Israel which is called to serve God's righteousness and make it known to all mankind is so defined that both Gentile and Jew have their rightful place in it. In chapters 12 to 15 Paul spells out the character of the new humanity and the new human community—the fruit of

God's justifying and reconciling work in Christ. We are warned, therefore, not to separate Romans 12 through 15 from the earlier chapters, as though they contained a code of Christian conduct which can stand independent of what has preceded it.

There are Christians who say, "Don't talk to me about justification by faith; just give me Romans 12 which tells me how to live as a Christian." The same people like to think that, in the Sermon on the Mount, Jesus has provided them with a set of rules for Christian living which permits them to bypass all the more profound questions of Christian belief. They want a simplified version of Christianity. What they are actually doing is turning a description of life in the new age—by Paul in Romans 12, or by Jesus in Matthew 5 through 7—into a new legal code, thereby making Christianity once more a religion in which men seek to justify themselves before God by their works. The life described here is not the life of people who are still their own masters. It is the life of those who have surrendered the mastery of their lives to Christ and who have received from him his own Spirit, the Spirit of self-effacing love, the Spirit of *God*, who alone, by his indwelling, is able to make man truly human.

The words in 12:1 which link Romans 12 to 15 closely with Romans 1—11 are "therefore" and "by the mercies of God." "Therefore" points back to all that God has done in Israel and finally in Jesus Christ to make possible the life of the new age. God's work through all the centuries has been a work of mercy and love toward his creation. He has sought to free it and all men from the power of evil and to prepare them for the life to which he had destined them. His crowning mercy is in the death and resurrection of Jesus. His death brought all mankind under judgment, and his resurrection opened to them the gates of a new world.

But the mercies of God call for a response from man. God's coming to man in Jesus Christ is fruitless unless it provokes a coming of man to God. God's gift of a new righteousness is actually the gift of himself to man and the gift has to be received with thanksgiving and joy, but also with obedience. Half-heartedness in the response means no real response, in fact no awareness of the greatness and costliness of the gift that is being offered. The only life worth having, the only truly human life is life in God, the life that broke upon the world in the person of Jesus and through him is opened to all mankind. But to have our life in God is to be possessed and mastered by the Spirit of God, not partially, not largely, but wholly. God gives himself to us, but to receive him we have to respond by giving ourselves to him. To "present your bodies as a living sacrifice" means "to present your selves," the self being understood as the totality of one's inward and outward life, not the inward without the outward and not the outward without the inward. But what is surrender of self to God except faith, the faith which Paul has been discussing from the beginning and the faith which, according to Jesus, so links God with man that it can move mountains?

In describing this faith as the sacrifice which is "holy and acceptable to God" and the Christian's "spiritual worship," Paul stands in continuity with the great prophets of Israel. Through the centuries the prophets had to contend with mistaken ideas of what constituted the true worship of God. Men found it easier to offer something other than themselves to God— an animal sacrifice (or even a human sacrifice), a beautiful ritual, a tithe of their income, a partial obedience—but the prophets insisted that the one true sacrifice was the humble and contrite heart, open unconditionally to God's will and proving its integrity by a step by step obedience. The worship of God is not something that

can be adequately cared for in a special place—
a special hour of the week, by a special rite or
ceremony, but is a worship that compasses the
whole self and the whole of life.

Verse 2 has the same comprehensiveness as
verse 1, picking up the earlier theme which pictured the Christian life as a movement out of
the age of sin and death into the new age of
righteousness and life. Paul had no illusions; he
knew that the Christian by his conversion did
not escape completely from the pull of the old
world. His new life had to be lived in the midst
of it, exposed constantly to the temptation to
fall back into its ways (compare Eph. 4, 5).
Everyone feels the pressure to conform to the
practices dominant in the society of which he is a
part, whether it has to do with the style of clothing or the style of life. Conformity in some respects is inescapable, if one is not to become a
laughable curiosity. But there is a point at which
conformity begins to mean the compromise of
one's faith, the giving up of the Christian venture toward the new age. Faith always has in it
rebellion against things as they are. To be in
Christ is to have the "mind" of Christ, to see all
things from a new vantage point, to do one's
thinking from a new center, so that, instead of
conforming easily, one is ready to probe into an

as yet undiscovered future to find what God's will has in store.

THE WELL-ORDERED COMMUNITY

We are reminded as we read 12:3-8 that Paul is writing not to individuals but to a church. Many people have made the Bible chiefly a book for private devotions. They listen for what it has to say to them as individuals and frequently miss what it says to them as members of a church community. If they looked more carefully at the character of the biblical writings in both Old and New Testaments, they would recognize that almost every part is addressed to the members of a community and is concerned with their relationships, first to God, then to each other, then to the world beyond their community. Our life is a life in relationships. We do not have a life in ourselves, apart from others, which we can change at will. We are webbed together with others. Our life is transformed only as our relationships with others in which we have our existence are transformed. We depend for our life not only upon God but also upon the people with whom our daily life brings us into contact.

Paul was aware that the constantly disruptive factor in life's relationships was human egotism, self-centeredness, pride, the drive of the self to be its own master. Long before Paul's time an ancient Hebrew writer had portrayed the essence of sin (Gen. 3) as the desire of man to be like God, i.e., to have no authority over him that would limit his freedom. The outcome of such unlimited and undisciplined freedom was anarchy and chaos, the destruction of community and so the self-destruction of man. Only the 'death,' or 'sacrifice' (12:1), of this natural self can open the way for a well-ordered human community. But so strong and persistent is the drive for self-realization that, even in a community of Christians who have died with Christ to sin and self, it (the ego factor) can continue to be a disruptive influence, expressing itself in the urge to capture a place of prominence in the fellowship. Therefore Paul, having called for a sacrifice of the whole self to God and having warned against conformity to the pattern of the old self-centered world, counsels the Roman Christians to exercise a true humility in determining what part each is to play in the life of the community.

Humility is a much-misunderstood Christian virtue. It is not a belittling of oneself before others but as Paul describes it here, a sober judgment concerning one's proper place in the community. The judgment must be based upon a recognition of the gifts with which faith has endowed the several members. A failure to use one's gifts is as reprehensible as an over-estimation of one's gifts. A false humility can be a cloak for timidity. We can be sure that faith has equipped every Christian with some capacity for the service of Christ. The healthy functioning of the community depends upon every member using his particular gifts, just as the healthy functioning of the human body depends upon every part of it doing its proper work. When some members begin to overestimate their importance and others decide that their efforts are really unimportant, degeneration sets in. We should note the emphasis Paul lays upon faith and grace (12:3,6) in forming a sound judgment in these matters. It is his way of saying that we can only form a right estimate of ourselves when we see ourselves and our relationships as they appear to us when we are in God's presence. *Grace* is God's presence with us, *faith* is our openness to him.

In verses 9-21 Paul issues a series of instructions concerning the attitudes of Christians to each other and their conduct in relation to non-Christians. It is not accidental that genuine love toward each other stands first. For Christians love is not just one virtue among others; it is the very core of their life in Christ. As Paul expresses it in another letter (I Cor. 13), love is so central to a Christian's existence that without it all else that he possesses is worthless. Faith is an openness to the love of God that lets his love flood in and become master in all life's relationships. Because it is a love that responds to God's love, it generates in the believer a hatred of evil and a love of whatever is good, so that one is impelled from within to obey the commandments which are rooted in respect for the neighbor (Rom. 13:8-10). Christian love is thus the fulfillment of the law. At first Romans 12:11-13 may seem to interrupt the theme of love with a series of brief incitements *not to be lacking in zeal,* or in *openness* to the Spirit, in *service,* in *joyful anticipation* of the future, *in patience under suffering,* in *persistence in prayer,* in *compassion for the needy,* or in *hospitality* toward fellow Christians. But each of these attitudes can be understood as an expression of love.

Paul takes up a fresh aspect of Christian love in verse 14, love toward the enemy, love which is tested most severely when the Christian has to face his persecutors. Paul does not anywhere suggest that the Roman church was being persecuted, but, from his own experience and the experience of his churches, he knew how the vigorous development of the Christian community could easily arouse fear and hatred in its neighbors. Before long he, himself, was to be a prisoner and then a martyr in Rome.

The *natural* response of any person to hatred and persecution was fear and hatred, but that only accentuated the evil and drove men farther apart. The Christian, however, has learned in Christ a different way of dealing with such evils: to respond to hatred with a love that looks beyond the hatred of the other person who, as a prisoner of his own fear and hatred, is debased by it. Love of this kind is the strongest weapon in the armory of the Christian in his battle for a new humanity. To respond to hatred with hatred is to lose the battle by becoming inhuman oneself. But to respond with love, and to continue to respond with love no matter how severe the offense, is to live in confidence of the ultimate victory.

In Christian churches which were confronted with a suspicious and hostile world, there must have been a tendency for members to draw back into themselves and live as closed communities, leaving the world to its own self-destruction. Such a withdrawal would be a betrayal of the Christian mission. The church existed as a community gathered and sent by God to invade the world for its redemption. It had, therefore, to be turned outward toward its neighbors, no matter how hostile they might be. Love for the neighbor outside was the spearhead of the invasion. We should understand verses 15-18, then, not as an appeal to Christians to show sympathy with each other, but rather as a demand that they lay themselves open to their non-Christian neighbors—to share their joys and sorrows, to live in harmony with them so far as possible; not to act as though they were superior to unbelievers, but to accept them as brothers and sisters.

This love for the outsider and the enemy was for Christians simply a reflection of the love of God which they themselves had experienced in Christ, a love that had accepted them when they were the ungodly, the outsiders, the enemy, so far as God was concerned. How could they receive the forgiving and reconciling love of God themselves unless they were willing to meet their neighbors with the same forgiving and reconciling love? To reinforce his argument Paul quotes a passage from the book of Proverbs (Prov. 25:21,22) which suggests that the only way to resist and to overcome evil is with 'good,' with love—by imitating the goodness and love of God.

Romans 13:1-7, with its doctrine that the Christian must show himself to be a loyal citizen, obedient to the lawful authorities in the state, may seem to interrupt Paul's discourse on love as the guiding principle of the church's life, especially when one notes that in verse 8 he returns directly to the theme of love. Some commentators have pointed out that Paul says nothing concerning citizenship that is distinctly Christian, nothing but what any loyal Roman citizen could have said: "Don't break the law, obey the government." Moreover, at no point does he seem to take account of the fact that there may be times when a Christian in his obedience to God may have to disobey the laws and decrees of the state. But we cannot disregard the context in which Romans 13:1-7 stands, for the Christian element in Paul's doctrine of citizenship resides chiefly in the context and must be sought there. The Christian's loyalty to the state is the direct fruit of his love for his neighbor, and his love for his neighbor is the fruit of God's love for him in Christ. He cannot have his life in Christ and not be committed to deal with his neighbors at all times in love, even though the neighbors, and the state which they constitute, may be hos-

VI

160

tile to him. The non-Christian may be a good citizen merely because he is a good Roman and as such wants to live in an orderly community; but the Christian is a good citizen for a profounder reason: he believes that the kind of love for others revealed in Christ is the one power able to transform the human community and eventually establish God's kingdom in the midst of men.

Paul has a second reason for counseling obedience to authority, and here he follows traditional Jewish teaching. Every government, he says, is instituted by God and he who resists the government resists what God has appointed. It is not difficult to see how a teaching such as this can be misused. Governments *have* misused it again and again to brand any attempt to overthrow them as contrary to biblical and Christian teaching. Can Paul be understood here as giving divine sanction to any and every government, no matter what its character may be? Are we to say that Hitler and Stalin, who in their time were the lawful authorities in their countries, had divine authority and that to resist them was to resist God? Were the thirteen colonies disobedient to God when they revolted against the existing British authority?

First, we must recognize that Paul does not

deal here with the problem of what the Christian must do when the state authority commands him to perform acts which are in contradiction to his loyalty to Jesus Christ. Paul was a Roman citizen with a healthy respect for Roman law and Roman administration of justice. More than once Roman officials had protected him from people who sought to harm him. With good reason he could counsel Christian churches to respect and obey such authorities and could see in them the working of God's providential care for all men. It was God's doing that in every community there were authorities which restrained the evil impulses of men and protected the welfare of all.

But there can be no doubt about what Paul's answer would have been had anyone asked him, "What shall we do if, in order to obey the government, we must be unfaithful to Christ?" The Christian life for Paul was life in Christ; to surrender to any influence which would separate the believer from Christ was for him unthinkable. It would mean nothing less than a reversion to the world of sin and death. It was not long before Roman Christians were to discover that unswerving obedience to Christ could mean disobedience to the Roman authorities, with severe persecution as a consequence.

Second, we must put Romans 13:1-7 in a still

larger biblical context. We find Jesus at an earlier date saying, as Paul did, that his followers should obey lawful authority and pay their taxes (Luke 20:25). There were Jews in Palestine who, in hatred of the Romans, refused to pay taxes and fomented rebellion. Jesus refused to make common cause with them. Yet there were some points at which Jesus came into collision with the religious authorities in his community since his teaching was contrary to theirs. When this happened he was so uncompromising that he stirred their fear and hatred. Eventually they crucified him as a rebel against the established order.

Again, in the Old Testament we find this more complex attitude to authority in the state. First the judge, and then the king, appears as God's appointee, chosen by God to guide and rule his people. To refuse obedience to him is to disobey God. But when the king is unfaithful in his office, when he no longer serves God's purposes for the nation, the prophet of God can proclaim his rejection and lead the people in rebellion against him. Thus, at one and the same time the prophetic faith could be both the strongest support of the state and a peril to its continuation in its existing form.

We need also to take account of the fact that

in the Book of Revelation the Roman state was represented as the very incarnation of the power of evil, the anti-Christ, when it became the intransigent persecutor of the Christian church. Paul must be seen, therefore, as contributing only one element to a Christian doctrine of the state. His principle of love for one's neighbor, in obedience to Christ, had in it (as a hidden implication) an implacable resistance to any authority in the state or elsewhere which might attempt to separate the Christian from Jesus Christ (cf. Rom. 8:38,39). Verses 8-10 make clear that Paul's concern has been with good citizenship as a necessary expression of love for the neighbor. Love fulfills both the law of God and the law of the state insofar as that law protects the welfare of all men and seeks their good.

The final verses, Romans 13:11-14, bring the whole question of Christian conduct into an eschatological perspective. Paul did not expect the present order to last much longer. Elsewhere (I Cor. 7:25-31) he counseled those who were not married not to enter into marriage since the time remaining would be so short. Soon the contradiction between the two ages would be at an end. The power of evil would be destroyed and the kingdom of God would be established throughout the whole creation. In comparison with that coming time of light and love, the present age is as night to day. The dawn is at hand. Therefore, Christians who have left a dying world behind and are living in joyful anticipation of God's new age must be awake and ready to enter more fully into its life. The "works of darkness," Paul knew were still a temptation to them. It was so easy to fall back into the corrupt practices of Roman society, since they had the approval of most men, but they were practices of a world from which men must be redeemed. The Christian must stand on God's side in the struggle between the forces of light and the forces of darkness. He must put on the armor of light; he must put on Christ and in oneness with Christ live for the coming day.

NO ROOM FOR DIVISIVE SELF-RIGHTEOUSNESS

In Romans 14:1-15:13 Paul focuses his attention upon a specific problem in the life of the church. In chapters 12 and 13 what he had to say could be applied to the Church generally in any place and any age, but in chapters 14 and 15 Paul seems to be dealing with a situation disrupting the fellowship in the Roman church, which had been brought to his notice. In letters such as those to Corinth or to Galatia we find Paul writing quite directly about the problems with which those particular churches were confronted, but for thirteen chapters in this letter to the Roman church the problems dealt with might be expected to appear in any church. It is surprising therefore that at this late point in the letter he should suddenly address himself to one special problem. We may assume that he had friends in Rome through whose letters he had received more information about the Roman church than chapters 1—13 indicate.

The situation is described very clearly. Differences in practice have arisen among those whom Paul recognizes as obedient in faith, and those differences are giving rise, on both sides, to attitudes of superiority, censoriousness, and exclusion. On the one hand some Christians with whom Paul frankly acknowledges his agreement, calling them the "strong" in faith (15:1), regard all things as clean, to be received as God's good gifts; they are free from the taboos which characterize religions which divide things into clean and unclean, sacred and secular. On the other hand there are Christians who refuse to eat meat or to drink wine, convinced that these have been forbidden them by God, and who regard some days as more sacred than others. Paul sees these practices as a sign of weakness in faith, a grasping for external supports.

Men who have arrived at the full maturity of faith in Christ have no need of such support and know that God has made all days and all things sacred and clean for the Christian. But the weakness is a weakness *in faith*. Not for a moment does Paul suggest that these people are depending on works and sacred observances rather than upon grace and faith for their salvation. What concerns him is that the strong in faith and the weak in faith are letting petty differences in practice become a wall of separation between them. More significant still, they are taking up self-righteous attitudes toward each other. This last development suggests why, at almost the close of his letter, Paul gives so much space to what seems at first to be quite a minor question. His theme has been the 'righteousness of *God*' which, as it becomes the life of man in the new creation, puts an end to all *human* pretensions of righteousness. The mark of the Christian is his freedom from all self-righteousness. Here, then, at the last, Paul is illustrating for his readers how easily the achievement of faith may be betrayed into a new form of self-righteousness. Human pride can in a moment change righteousness into self-righteousness and disrupt the fellowship that faith has brought into being.

Paul's insistence that differences of the kind

indicated here are to be tolerated within the community of faith must not be interpreted as an easy tolerance on his part of all differences in belief and practice. Had there been any suggestion that man's salvation was dependent upon his refraining from meat and wine and observing certain holy days, he would have seen the truth of the gospel endangered and would have protested sharply. But no such issue was involved in the situation. The difference was like the difference between John the Baptist and Jesus, John practicing a rigorous asceticism and Jesus enjoying food and wine with his friends. When it was suggested to Jesus that he should conform to John's model, Jesus replied that each of them must be left free to serve God in his own way (Luke 7:31-35).

As chapter 14 opens, Paul's theme is still (as in Romans 12 and 13) the rule of love in the Christian fellowship. Those who are strong in faith are to receive those who differ from them in practice and not allow the differences to disrupt the unity of their life together. Those who are ascetic in their attitude to food and drink are not to think the others less earnest in their faith than themselves. If God accepts both, not because of anything that they do, but simply in his love for them, receiving them in their unworthiness when they respond to him in faith, then surely they can accept each other and live together in the service of God's kingdom. To sit in judgment on one another is disobedience to God for it is a rejection of what God has accepted. Paul (14:5ff) introduces a conditioning note. The practices are acceptable only if and when they are an expression of faith (cf. v. 23). Both freedom and restraint in eating and drinking must be acts of obedience, performed in honor of the Lord—for this is the mark of the Christian, that in all he does in life and in death he serves the purpose for which Christ died and rose again, the coming of the new age in which eventually every knee shall bow to him as Lord.

Paul then moves to a new consideration (Rom. 14:11). In a community where love prevails, *the strong will accept limitations on their freedom in order to protect the weak.* The person who considers it wrong to eat meat or to drink wine may be led astray by the example of his stronger brother and may thereby suffer serious injury. Paul does not call on the strong to become vegetarians or abstainers but only to exercise care that their freedom in regard to food and drink may do no injury to other Christians. The strong must maintain a Christian perspective in these matters. What real difference does it make whether they have their meat and wine if the spiritual welfare of some of their fellow Christians is at stake? What matters above all else is the progress of the Kingdom; no obstacle must be allowed to hinder its advance. Food and drink are minor concerns in comparison with righteousness, peace, and joy in the Holy Spirit. God's great work takes precedence over all else and in every moment. The obedience of faith is a readiness to do whatever may be necessary to set it forward.

Paul continues his plea for unity in the church in chapter 15:1-13 and anchors his plea in the example of Christ, who in his life and death sought not his own pleasure but the welfare of others. The Christian life is life in Christ, dying with him to the old world of self in order to rise with him into the new world of God's grace and love (6:4). If Christ receives men into such fellowship with himself, how can they do other than receive one another and live in harmony to the glory of the God and Father of Jesus Christ? The continuity of Paul's thought in verses 8-12 is somewhat obscure. Why does he distinguish Jew (the circumcised) and Gentile here? The point may be that just as Christ by humbling himself to be the servant of his Jewish people made possible the fulfillment of the promise of the Old Testament—that Gentiles and Jews would one day be united in the service of the one true God—so now an imitation of his humility by Christians could dissolve the lesser barriers between the strong and the weak in the church at Rome. Paul concludes his appeal for unity with a prayer (v. 13) which, by its emphasis upon hope, encourages the Roman Christians to live with all their energies focused on the coming of the new day.

PAUL'S CONCLUDING PERSONAL REMARKS

Paul hastens in Romans 15:14 to remove any impression that he thinks the Roman Christians are in need of instruction from him, just as he did in 1:12. He is confident that they understand the gospel quite well enough to instruct one another and even to give him some encouragement in faith. However, he has made bold to remind them of certain essential points because he has received from God a special responsibility for the preaching of the gospel to the Gentiles, and for the offering of the Gentiles to God as a holy and acceptable sacrifice. It is surprising that Paul does not say, as he does in the letter to the Galatians, that he is *the* apostle to the Gentiles, commissioned by Christ himself for this service and recognized as such by the Jerusalem church. But as yet there has been no challenge to his authority in Rome as there was in the Galatian church. His approach throughout the letter has been to claim authority not for himself but for the truth of the gospel. He is content to have referred to his apostleship in chapter 1 and to speak of himself here only as "a minister of Christ Jesus to the Gentiles." However, what Christ has already achieved through him among the Gentiles is a validation of his ministry. He has covered a territory which stretches all the way from Jerusalem to the west coast of Greece (Illyricum), making it his principle to preach where the gospel has not yet been heard. The Roman church belongs in a different category and therefore calls for a different approach on his part. But beyond Rome and as far west as Spain there is territory that is yet to be conquered for Christ, and Paul wants the Roman church to become the base for this western campaign (just as the Antioch church was the base for the missions in the Eastern Mediterranean area). It would be some time before Paul could begin this new mission for he had first to return to Jerusalem with the fund gathered for the relief of the Jerusalem poor (vv. 25-29). But with that task finished, he assures them that he will visit them on his way to Spain.

Paul's letter ends with a request that the Roman Christians join with him in prayers for the success of his Jerusalem mission. Paul was still regarded as an arch-traitor to his own nation by many of his fellow Jews in Jerusalem. He knew how dangerous it was for him to go within reach of them. He seems also to have been somewhat uncertain how he would be received by the Jerusalem Christians. They might resent his coming as likely to disturb their peaceful relations with their non-Christian Jewish brethren. But, it was worth the risk if the generosity of the Gentile churches should help to form a bond of unity between Gentile and Jew. Paul was not one to shrink from any danger when the welfare of the worldwide Christian fellowship was at stake. Then, with that hill surmounted, he would have the joy of his first meeting with the church in Rome. He little knew that the journey to Rome would be made in chains!

LOVE FULFILLS BOTH THE LAW OF GOD
AND THE LAW OF THE STATE
INSOFAR AS THAT LAW PROTECTS
THE WELFARE OF ALL MEN AND
SEEKS THEIR GOOD.   [164]

THE CHRISTIAN IS A GOOD CITIZEN FOR
A PROFOUND REASON: HE BELIEVES THAT THE KIND OF LOVE FOR
OTHERS REVEALED IN CHRIST IS THE ONE POWER ABLE TO
TRANSFORM THE HUMAN COMMUNITY AND EVENTUALLY ESTAB-
LISH GOD'S KINGDOM IN THE MIDST OF MEN.   [161]

FOR CHRISTIANS,
LOVE IS NOT ONE VIRTUE AMONG OTHERS;
IT IS THE VERY CORE OF THEIR LIFE IN CHRIST. [156]

FAITH IS AN OPENNESS TO THE LOVE OF GOD
THAT LETS HIS LOVE FLOOD IN
AND BECOME MASTER IN ALL LIFE'S RELATION-
SHIPS.   [157]

NOTES

1. William Wrede, *Paul* (Naperville, Ill.: American Theological Library Association, reprinted by Alec R. Allenson, Inc., 1962).

2. Quite recently scholars have been giving special attention to the theological standpoint of the authors of the gospels, recognizing that they were not just literary editors of the traditions but also theological interpreters, e.g.,

   Hanz Conzelmann, *The Theology of Saint Luke* (London: Faber & Faber, 1960).

3. For the problems in interpreting the Book of Acts two collections of essays are very helpful:

   Martin Dibelius, *Studies in the Acts of the Apostles* (New York: Scribners, 1956).

   L. Keck and L. Martyn, *Studies in Luke—Acts* (Nashville: Abingdon, 1966).

4. See Keck and Martyn, *Studies in Luke—Acts.*

5. Acts 11.   6. Gal. 2:12 ff.

7. The conditions for sharing the apostolate according to the author of Acts are stated in Acts 1:21, 22. Paul does not meet such conditions.

8. Gal 1:11, 12.   9. Acts 9:26 ff., cf. Gal. 1:18 ff.   10. Gal. 2:7-9.

11. Martin Dibelius, *Studies in the Acts of the Apostles,* has a thorough discussion of this question.

12. Karl Barth, *Der Römerbrief* (Bern: G. A. Baschlin, 1918).

13. Karl Barth, *Epistle to the Romans* (New York: Oxford University Press, 1933). (Original German first edition 1922.)

14. C. K. Barrett, *Epistle to the Romans* (New York: Harper & Row, 1958).

15. W. C. Van Unnik, *Tarsus or Jerusalem, the City of Paul's Youth* (Naperville, Ill.: Allenson, 1952).

   Van Unnik has, by an analysis of Acts 22:3, shown this to be the most likely sequence of events in the childhood and youth of Paul.

16. C. A. Anderson Scott, *Romanism and the Gospel* (Phila.: Westminster Press, 1937).

17. C. K. Barrett, *Epistle to the Romans,* offers a clear discussion of this problem.

18. Isa. 45:8; 46:13; 51:6, etc.   19. Psalm 24:5; 36:10; 103:17, etc.

20. An examination of Paul's quotations of the Old Testament shows that he usually read his Old Testament in a Greek translation.

BOOKS

Commentaries especially useful and readable, with differing approaches, are:

BARRETT, CHARLES K. *The Epistle to the Romans.* New York: Harper & Row, 1958.

NYGREN, ANDERS. *Commentary on Romans.* Translated by Carl C. Rasmussen. Phila.: Fortress Press, 1949.

BARTH, KARL. *A Shorter Commentary on Romans.* Richmond, Va.: John Knox Press, 1959, out of print.

KNOX, JOHN. *Romans.* The Interpreter's Bible, vol. IX. Nashville: Abingdon, 1954.

Luther's commentary, which greatly influenced John Wesley, has a valuable introduction in:

LUTHER, MARTIN. *Luther: Lectures on Romans.* Translated and edited by Wilhelm Pauck. Library of Christian Classics, Vol. XV. Phila.: Westminster, 1961.

Barth's larger commentary had a profound influence when published in 1922:

BARTH, KARL. *Epistle to the Romans.* Translated by Sir Edwyn C. Hoskyns. New York: Oxford University Press, 6th ed., 1933. (Paper, 1968.)

The literature on various aspects of Romans and on Paul is vast and presents a wide variety of viewpoints. Two books which are indispensable in studying Paul in Acts are:

> DIBELIUS, MARTIN. *Studies in the Acts of the Apostles.* New York: Scribner's, 1956; out of print.

> KECK, LEANDER E. and J. LOUIS MARTYN (joint editors). *Studies in Luke—Acts.* Nashville: Abingdon, 1966, out of print.

> GRIFFITH, A. LEONARD. *The Roman Letter Today.* Nashville: Abingdon Press, 1959, out of print.

This interesting, compact book, in addition to sixty pages on Romans, includes other letters by Paul:

> SCOTT, C. A. ANDERSON. *Footnotes to Saint Paul.* Cambridge: Cambridge University Press, 1931, out of print.

This is a very good book on Paul's letters:

> SCOTT, C. A. ANDERSON. *Christianity According to Saint Paul.* Cambridge: Cambridge University Press. (Paper.)

The following works may be studied in relation to the influence of the *Letter to the Romans* on the thinking of John Wesley:

> CLARK, ELMER T. *What Happened At Aldersgate.* Nashville: Methodist Publishing House, 1938, out of print.

> WESLEY, JOHN. *Journals of John Wesley.* Vol. 1. New York: Eaton & Mains, 1909.

AUTHOR

JAMES DICK SMART, Jesup Professor of Biblical Interpretation at Union Theological Seminary in New York City 1957-1971, is one of the most distinguished and influential Christian writers and thinkers of North America. Born in Ontario, Canada, Dr. Smart was ordained to the Presbyterian ministry in 1931. His pastorates include Rosedale Presbyterian Church in Toronto.

A prolific writer and lecturer, Dr. Smart has helped shape the curriculum in church schools in both the United States and Canada. From 1944 to 1950, he was editor-in-chief for the Board of Christian Education of the Presbyterian Church in the U.S.A., setting up its new curriculum: "Christian Faith and Life." He served as lecturer in homiletics and Christian education in Knox College, Toronto, Ontario, before coming to Union Theological Seminary in 1957.

Dr. Smart received B.A., M.A. and Ph.D. degrees from the University of Toronto and did post graduate work at the Universities of Marburg and Berlin, Germany. Dr. Smart married Miss Christine McKillop. They have three daughters. Dr. Smart is a frequent lecturer and preacher in theological seminaries and on college campuses in the United States and Canada and has given the Carnahan lectures at Union Seminary in Buenos Aires.

A member of the Society of Biblical Literature and Exegesis and an editor of the Westminster Study Edition of the Holy Bible, Dr. Smart's writings include the following books:

The ABC's of Christian Faith, The Divided Mind of Modern Theology: Karl Barth and Rudolf Bultmann, 1908-1933, History and Theology in Second Isaiah: A Commentary on Isaiah 35, 40-66, The Interpretation of Scripture, A Promise to Keep, The Quiet Revolution: The Radical Impact of Jesus on Men of His Time, The Rebirth of Ministry, Servants of the Word: The Prophets of Israel (Westminster Guides to the Bible), The Strange Silence of the Bible in the Church: A Study in Hermeneutics, The Teaching Ministry of the Church: An Examination of the Basic Principles of Christian Education, What a Man Can Believe.

In DOORWAY TO A NEW AGE Dr. Smart writes that, "Paul's letter to the Romans must be read, reread, and pondered, until it ceases to be a letter to some Roman Christians of long ago and becomes a personal letter from Paul to *you!*" And he reminds us that, "More than once in the past this letter to the Romans has led Christians to rediscover the power of the New Testament faith to shake their world and to transform it."

Dr. Smart now makes his headquarters at Islington, Ontario in Canada, where he continues his writing between speaking and teaching engagements. On a part time basis he is co-pastor of Rosedale Presbyterian Church in Toronto.

WHEN SOME MEMBERS
BEGIN TO OVERESTIMATE THEIR IMPORTANCE
AND OTHERS DECIDE THAT THEIR EFFORTS
ARE REALLY UNIMPORTANT,
DEGENERATION SETS IN. [156]

LONG BEFORE PAUL'S TIME AN ANCIENT HEBREW WRITER
HAD PORTRAYED THE ESSENCE OF SIN (GEN. 3) AS
THE DESIRE OF MAN TO BE LIKE GOD—
TO HAVE NO AUTHORITY OVER HIM
THAT WOULD LIMIT HIS FREEDOM. [155]

FAITH IS OUR OPENNESS
TO GOD'S ACTION. [67]

A CHRISTIAN CHURCH THAT HAS NOT YET
DEALT FORCEFULLY WITH THE PROBLEM OF ITS OWN MEMBERS'
HOSTILITY TO JEWS IS HARDLY CREDIBLE AS A MESSENGER OF
GOD'S LOVE FOR MANKIND AS REVEALED IN JESUS CHRIST. [127]

THE KINGDOM OF HEAVEN
WHOSE NEARNESS JESUS ANNOUNCED,
WAS YET TO COME.
BUT IT WAS ALREADY PRESENT
AS A NEW ORDER OR DIMENSION OF LIFE
IN WHICH GOD'S PRESENCE
COULD BE KNOWN NOW.
[102]

GLOSSARY

ANTIPATHY — Dislike or hostility.

ANTITHESIS — Something which stands at the opposite pole; contrast.

ANTITHETICAL— Opposite in character; directly opposing.

ASCETICISM—A form of religious devotion which severely limits all physical satisfactions; strict self-denial for the sake of a higher spiritual or intellectual state.

AURA—The manifestation of a presence conceived as given off by the person concerned; subtle, invisible manifestation of presence or atmosphere.

AUTHENTIC—Genuine; in accord with fact or actuality; trustworthy.

BROKENLY—Imperfectly; partially.

CASTIGATES—Rebukes scorchingly.

CASTIGATION—Violent condemnation.

CENSORIOUSNESS— Harsh criticism and condemnation.

CHRIST EVENT, THE —A comprehensive term to describe the whole of God's action in Jesus for our salvation, both in his ministry, including his death, and in his risen power, in and through his church.

CODA—Concluding passage or phrase of music.

COMMENSURATE— In keeping with; equal in measure.

COMMENTATORS— Biblical scholars who interpret the Scriptures.

CONFESSIONAL CHURCH—The church which in Germany, in 1934, confessed that its first loyalty in all things must be to Jesus Christ and which refused to bow to Nazi rule.

CONSTITUENCY—A distinctive section of the population.

CONSUMMATION— Completion; fulfillment.

CONTENTIOUSLY— In a quarreling spirit.

DETERMINISTIC— Any view of human life

which regards events as determined beforehand; either by God, by fate, or just by the flow of history.

DIASPORA—The Jewish population scattered across the world from 722 B.C. on.

DISPARAGE—Belittle.

DISPERSION—The Jewish population living outside Palestine.

DIVERGE—Go apart.

ENCLAVE—The enclosure formed by Jewish exclusiveness.

ERA—A span of time, an age.

184 ESCHATOLOGICAL—Having to do with the final outcome of human history and destiny.

EXISTENTIALISM—A modern philosophy which attempts to translate all statements into expressions of man's understanding of himself and his world.

EXORCISE—Drive out (Christ drove out the evil spirits from the epileptic) .

EXPIATION—An act which cancels the power of sin to separate a man from God.

EXPRESSION—Statement; formulation.

FAITH—The liberating response of a man's whole being to God's gracious acceptance of him in and through Jesus Christ.

FLESHLY—Paul uses flesh with two different meanings. Sometimes the term denotes *the world that is under the tyranny of sin;* but at other times it means only our *physical existence as human beings.*

GRACE—God's graciousness and care for us in ministering to our needs through Jesus Christ.

HERITAGE—The beliefs, values, traditions, and institutions transmitted to the present by one's history and by those who have gone before.

HYPOTHESIS—A tentative theory to explain facts, and to guide investigation.

IMPERVIOUS—totally resistant; unmoved.

INCARNATION—An Event in which the presence of God becomes wholly real in the existence of a human being.

INTERJECTION—A phrase or remark abruptly inserted in the middle of a sentence or statement.

INTRANSIGENT—Uncompromising; unwilling to change or adjust.

IRENIC—peaceful; promoting peaceful relations.

IRRELIGIOUS—Disregard or disrespect for religion.

ISRAEL—Descendants of Jacob; God's chosen people.

JUSTIFICATION—Our acceptance into fellowship with God in spite of the sins which make us unworthy; therefore forgiveness and reconciliation are included. It is made possible only by what God does for us in Jesus Christ.

KOSHER—Foods permitted to a Jew, chosen and prepared in accordance with Old Testament laws.

METAPHOR—A word or phrase used in place of another to say the same thing more vividly.

NEGATE—Deny; oppose.

NIRVANA—A state of freedom from passion and illusion—attainment of an inner peace.

PAR EXCELLENCE—In its highest form.

PENTATEUCH—The first five books of the Old Testament.

PITCH—Level.

POSTHUMOUS—After death; something which takes place after the death of the person concerned.

PREDESTINATION—The belief that God has a purpose for our life and for the world's life that works itself out in our history.

PROPHETS—Those inspired by God to speak forth in his name.

PROTAGONIST—Aggressive representative.

PUBLICAN—A tax collector for the Romans, scorned and hated by his fellow Jews.

REALIST—One who recognizes the true state of things in life and cherishes no illusions.

RECONCILIATION—The overcoming of alienation, hostility, and separation of persons.

REDEMPTION—
Rescue of man from evil and restoration of fellowship with God and man.

RELIGIOSITY—
Extreme and false piety; the diligent practice of religious forms without any real understanding of the reality of faith.

SADISTIC—The pleasure or enjoyment of human suffering, whether inflicted on one's self or on someone else.

SALVATION—The realization in human life, individual and social, of God's gracious purpose.

SOCIETY—Community; people united by association or for common ends.

SPECULATIVE—Conjecturing without sufficient evidence.

TORAH—The Hebrew word for law; used first as the title of the first five books of the Old Testament but sometimes extended to include the whole of the Old Testament.

TRADITIONS—The oral form in which much of both the Old and New Testaments was transmitted from generation to generation before being finally fixed in a written form.

TRAVAIL—A condition of struggle and suffering, as in the pain of childbirth.

WORD—At the center of Scripture is the conviction that God has made himself and his will for man known in definite words, heard by a series of men, remembered and recorded, but these words become God's word ever afresh to future generations only as in them God himself confronts them and speaks to their situation.

ZEALOTRY—Earnest devotion, extreme zeal verging on fanaticism; Zealots, Jewish sect bitterly opposed to Roman domination of Palestine.

ABBREVIATIONS

A.D.— (Latin: anno Domini) —In the year of our Lord.

ARV—American Standard Revised Version of the Bible.

B.C.—Before Christ.

ca.— (Latin: circa) — about, approximately.

cf.—Compare.

e.g.— (Latin: *exempli gratia*) —for example.

f.—Following (verse or page) ; ff.—Following (verses or pages).

ibid.—The same book.

i.e.— (Latin: *id est*) — That is; for example.

KJV—King James Version of the Bible.

op. cit.—In the work [book] mentioned earlier.

p.—Page; pp.—pages.

RSV—Revised Standard Version of the Bible.

seq.—And following.

viz.— (Latin: *videlicet*) — Namely.

v.—Verse; vv.—verses.

vs.—Versus.

NO MATTER HOW GREAT THE POWER OF SIN MAY BE,
THE POWER OF GRACE IS GREATER.   [85]

TEMPTATION AND SIN REMAIN A
PROBLEM FOR THE CHRISTIAN TO THE
VERY END OF HIS JOURNEY.   [88]

LET US CEASE TO KNOW THAT WE ARE
SINNERS IN A WORLD DESPERATELY IN NEED OF REDEMPTION—
AND ALL TOO QUICKLY WE SHALL BE ANCHORED IN COMPLA-
CENCY.   [100]

THIS IS THE MIRACLE OF GRACE, THAT
CHRIST TAKES US, SINNERS THAT WE ARE, INTO THE RICHNESS AND
JOY AND BOUNDLESS HOPE OF HIS OWN LIFE IN GOD.   [108]

A POWER IS AT WORK IN THE CHRISTIAN
TO OVERCOME SIN AND
TO BRING RIGHTEOUSNESS INTO
ALL HUMAN RELATIONS [88]

QUESTIONS FOR STUDY

Chapter I

1. Compared with other New Testament authors, where have you usually rated Paul as a witness to the Christ Event?

2. What difference does it make whether we begin with the letters of Paul or with Acts in forming our picture of Paul?

3. What features of Paul's letter to the Romans account for the fact that for Luther, John Wesley, Karl Barth, and countless others it opened the way to a fresh understanding of the gospel? What were the consequences of their study of Romans in their lives? in the church? in society?

189

4. Why should a strong influence of the Jerusalem church upon the church at Rome tend to cause criticism and distrust of Paul and his gospel?

5. Why is the letter to the Romans so different from other letters, such as those to the Corinthians and the Galatians?

6. Many people today think that differences in the interpretation of Christianity should be ignored in the interests of unity. Paul, in Romans, brings one such difference into the open and speaks to it. What would have been the result if he had failed to challenge a strongly legalistic version of the Christian faith? Do we face any equally serious differences?

Chapter II

1. If Paul was already an earnestly religious and moral person before he became a Christian, what difference did his relationship with Jesus Christ make in him?

2. Can you conceive of an earnestly religious and moral person needing to be radically converted? Do you know such persons? Are you one?

3. In what way can our religion and virtue become the basis of a self-righteousness and a sense of self-justification before God, and make us deaf to any further claim he might make upon us?

4. What three different meanings can be conveyed by the term 'the righteousness of God'?

5. Have you ever felt ashamed of your faith? If so, why?

6. Do we expect people to understand easily the words in which the Christian gospel is expressed? Why is there difficulty?

7. What are the dimensions of salvation in Paul's thought?

8. How does the biblical definition of sin differ from the conceptions of it which are most common in our minds?

9. Why has 'justification by faith' seemed to some men to be an encouragement of immorality? What do you think?

10. Is Paul twisting the Old Testament to his purpose or giving it its proper interpretation when he

finds 'justification by faith' rooted in Abraham and the Psalms?

11. What difference, if any, does your faith make in your attitude and actions concerning suffering, hunger, injustice, and other evils?

Chapter III

1. What are some of the meanings of the word 'faith' in current usage?

2. What difference does it make to the content of faith when it is faith in Christ crucified and risen?

3. Is Jesus just one significant factor in the varied history of the human race or can we still agree with Paul that he forms the crux between two eras which are opposed—two antithetical orders of life?

4. How responsible was Israel's vision of a coming kingdom of justice, mercy, and peace, for the constant prophetic ferment of revolt against the established order?

a) Today, how responsible is a Christian's vision of the kingdom of heaven for the revolt of youth against laws and privileges and institutions which perpetuate inequities and the monopolies of the rich?

b) Give some examples of injustices which exist today.

c) Give some examples of changes in laws today of which Christ would approve.

5. What is man's real nature: sinner or man in Christ? Which is the real world: the world broken by

its sin or the world healed and restored by the coming of the Kingdom? What does it mean, then, to be a realist?

6. What is the relation between the inward journey of our faith and our outward progress in the world?

7. What can a 'cheap' peace of mind do to the Christian's journey of faith?

   a) Does a Christian have an easy life?
   b) What insurance for a peaceful, painless life does being a Christian provide?

8. Why does the Cross set us in motion from an old world to a new?

   a) What was the meaning of the Cross? What is its meaning today?
   b) Why is an understanding of its meaning so powerful in the changing of lives?
   c) Does a full understanding of the meaning of the Cross and the personal acceptance of it in one's own experience result in a different way of thinking and doing?

9. What does baptism mean to you—a name-giving ceremony, a dedication of a child to God, a symbol of the Christian's willingness to die with Christ to the world of sin and to rise with him into a new life in God? (Dare a parent commit his child to this latter choice?)

Chapter IV

1. What words most puzzle you in your reading of Romans? Make a list of them and clarify their mean-

ing, using the text, GLOSSARY (p. 183), dictionaries, and discussions.

2. What different names for the Scriptures are used in the New Testament?

3. How conscious are you of the blending of American culture and Christian faith in yourself? in people about you? in public statements by national spokesmen, past and present? Can you give examples?

4. In what way can Christianity become a new form of legalism?

5. In what way will Jesus Christ, if he is truly known, bring "not peace but a sword" into the life of our congregations? Into my life?

6. Should a Christian be beyond the kind of inner struggle which Paul describes in Romans 7:14-24?

7. What in our national experience would cause God's wrath? What evidences of it do you see today? In our city?

8. To what extent is our freedom from suffering as Christians in America purchased at the cost of concealment and evasion of the problems which point up the conflict between the gospel and the cherished values of our communities? What are some of these conflicts in a five-mile radius of your church?

9. Are you willing to force issues into the open when such "faithfulness" to Christ will be dangerous and/or costly?

10. How does 'life in the Spirit' create a new sense of responsibility for man's total life-environment?

11. What are the implications of 'life in the Spirit' for our national life? for our international relations?

12. Is your church turned inward on itself or turned outward toward the world?

13. What are the expressions of the "eager longing" of the creation for its freedom from death and decay? What is your personal responsibility, as members of the church, in this respect?

Chapter V

1. What is the relation between the widespread abandonment of the Old Testament by many Christians and the equally widespread indifference to the relation between the Church and Judaism?

2. What is your attitude toward the Jewish people? Toward the Jews with whom you come in personal contact?

3. What are the ways you can list by which Jews are discriminated against? How can the face of Christ or the teachings of Christ be made evident?

4. If the call of God is irrevocable and the Jews are still his chosen people—together with the Christian church—what should be the relationship between church and synagogue, between Christians and Jews?

5. Why is a special mission to convert the Jews a highly questionable enterprise?

6. What is the relation of the Church to historical Judaism? What should it be?

7. Ask someone to review related points from *The Invitation,* the study of Matthew by Hans-Ruedi Weber.

Chapter VI

1. What happens to the Christian faith and to Christians when they try to reduce that faith to a set of rules for Christian living?

2. How does a Christian determine the point at which he must refuse to conform to the accepted practices of the world in which he lives? To what extent must this refusal to conform make him a rebel against the established order?

3. What is the relation between the centrality of love in the Christian life and the definition of a Christian as one who has received the Holy Spirit?

4. Why is love for the outsider and the enemy essential to a Christianity that stands under the sign of the Cross?

5. Is it a misuse of Romans 13:1-7 to interpret it as demanding that Christians should give unquestioning obedience to their government?

6. What differences in practices serve as a basis for divisive attitudes of superiority and self-righteousness among modern Christians?

7. Do you know of such divisive attitudes toward other churches or members of your own church?

8. Do you give love, forgiveness and help to anyone regardless of race, creed, denomination, enmity, or wrongdoing? Whose faith and courage in our day can you compare with that of Paul and his fellow Christians?

9. What is the difference between good citizenship that is the expression of Christian faith and love and

good citizenship which is simply an expression of loyalty to one's own nation or community?

10. Do you know of anyone willing to die with Christ for others?

11. Do you know of anyone willing to endure prison for their Christian faith?

196